RECORD TOOLS

A Reprint of Catalogue No 15 of 1938
With a Guide for Plane Collectors

by

Leslie Harrison

Roy Arnold

This edition first published in 2003

by

*Roy Arnold
77 High Street
Needham Market
Suffolk IP6 8AN*

ISBN 978-0-904638-14-1

Introduction © 2003 by Leslie Harrison

All rights reserved. Except for brief quotations in a review the text of this book or any part thereof may not be produced or transmitted in any form without written permission from the publisher.

A CIP Catalogue record for this book is available from the British Library

Text set in Georgia

INTRODUCTION

When the brothers Charles and Joseph Hampton moved to Sheffield, from Wednesbury in the Midlands, in the closing years of the 19th century, they could not have realised that the company they were to establish was to become one of Britain's best known manufacturers of hand tools for the engineering and woodworking industries, which was later to become better known by its trademark of Record.

When founded in 1898, C & J Hampton, as the company was then known, produced a variety of items which the industries of the period demanded. Marlin spikes, jacks, flywheel and specialist castings were listed as being manufactured. When C & J Hampton became a limited company in 1908 their premises were located at Eagle Foundry, Livingston Road, Sheffield and it was at this address, one year later, that the Record trademark was registered in the *Trade Mark Journal*.

> 313,863-4655 S. Unwrought and Partly Wrought Metals used in Manufacture. C. & J. Hampton, Limited, Eagle Foundry, Livingstone *(sic)* Road, Sheffield: Engineers, Ironfounders and General Tool Manufacturers-10th June 1909.

In the first decade of the 20th century a decision was taken to concentrate on hand tool manufacture. This proved to be sound policy as the industrial demand for hand tools at that time was immense and they formed the basis of the company's product range for a century. Between 1909 and 1930 the mainstay of production consisted of engineering and woodworking vices, G cramps, sash and T- bar cramps, floor cramps, pipe vices, pipe cutters, Stillson pattern pipe wrenches and lifting jacks. By 1912 the company had relocated to a new factory at Ouse Road, Attercliffe, Sheffield.

Catalogues

In catalogue No 10 of January 1931, Record introduced a range of woodworking planes which they marketed as an entirely new British product. Government import tariffs of the late 1920's assisted British manufacturers in combating the influx of foreign manufactured planes, mainly from the U.S.A., which at that time dominated the market. A "Buy British" campaign was launched to combat the depression in the United Kingdom during that period.

Catalogue No 11 followed in September 1932 with new lines in hand drills and bolt clippers being introduced. New model numbers in planes and spokeshaves also appeared.

Catalogues Nos 12 and 12A of 1933 and 1934 respectively added more planes to the range and a new line in hand and breast drills. There was no catalogue No 13 issued.

Catalogue No 14 of November 1935 listed 25 additional patterns of plane which included spokeshaves and a range of 9 different weights of brass plumb bob.

Catalogue No 15, published in February 1938, probably represented the peak of pre-World War 2 production. By this time extra premises had been secured at Bernard Road, Sheffield for a head office and branch factory.

In 1939 a range of 11 carpenters' braces was introduced. Although these featured in several price lists and a publicity leaflet, they never appeared in any catalogues and were listed as 'temporarily out of production' in 1944 due to pressures of the war effort. They did not make a re-appearance.

Catalogue No 16 issued in 1949 contained virtually the same tools as No 15 but the accompanying price list showed that many tools appearing in the catalogue were out of production because of wartime or post-war manufacturing restrictions. Many of the suspended products never made it back into production. Throughout the 1950's and up to 1963, catalogue No 16 was re-issued in pocket form frequently to keep post-war customers informed of the availability of tools and new ones as and when they were introduced. Updated price lists were issued when necessary.

Catalogue No 17 was issued in large format in 1963 when the company moved into a new factory at Parkway Works. No 17 catalogue was re-issued in pocket size form until circa 1970.

Catalogue No 18 was issued in 1972 when C & J Hampton Ltd merged with William Ridgway Ltd, who manufactured wood boring tools, to become Record-Ridgway Tools Ltd. Subsequent catalogues were not numbered.

In March 1981 A B Bahco of Sweden bought the company and a new company emerged in 1985 called Record Holdings which purchased Record-Ridgway Ltd. The name Record Marples (Woodworking Tools) Ltd applied from 1988. The last decade of the 20th century saw three more company name changes: Record Tools Ltd in 1991, Record Holdings plc in 1993 and currently Record Tools Ltd (a division of American Tool Companies Inc) since 1998.

Throughout the mergers and take-overs of the late 20th century the company have continued to produce quality tools to the current day. Some products have changed, some have been deleted and new ones have been introduced to meet the demands of modern industry and the individual user, but the name of Record is still widely recognised as a benchmark by which many quality hand tools are measured.

Dates for Introduction of Planes in Catalogues and Price Lists

The following dates at which various patterns of plane were introduced have been obtained from company catalogues, price lists, publicity leaflets and the various editions of the book *Planecraft*, which C & J Hampton Ltd first published in 1934 to enhance the knowledge of planes of the woodworkers of the day. Dates are accurate to within approximately one year. Companies very often had new products in the shops before they appeared in their catalogue. In this respect publicity leaflets distributed to tool shops could inform prospective purchasers of a new tool which would be included in the next catalogue when it was published.

Record chose to manufacture a well established range of iron planes which had already passed through most of the evolutionary process and which had become accepted by the British woodworker of the time. The range was based on the planes manufactured by Stanley in the U.S.A. which, by 1930, had passed their expiry date for patent protection, thereby allowing any competitor to copy their products without patent infringement.

Stanley dominated the iron plane market in the U.S.A. and in the late 19th century viewed Britain as another customer to be won over from using wooden and transitional type planes. How successful C & J Hampton were in winning sales of planes from Stanley is not known, but import tariffs on foreign manufactured planes and the encouragement for purchasers to buy British goods manufactured by British labour must have proved very encouraging to Record. The number of plane patterns offered increased quickly over a 6 year period as will be observed from the following catalogue and price lists.

<u>January 1931 – Catalogue No 10</u>
Bench Planes: 03, 04, 04½, 05, 05½, 06, 07, 08
Block Planes: 0110, 0120, 0220

<u>September 1932 – Catalogue No 11</u>
Block Planes: 0102, 0130, 0230. Rebate Planes: 010, 010½, 078, 075. Plough Planes: 050. Routers: 071, 071½. Circular Planes: 020, 0113. Scraper Planes: 070, 080. Spokeshaves: 051, 051R, 053, 055, 063, 064, 0151, 0151R

<u>August 1933 – Price List</u>
Bench Plane: 02. Rebate Planes: 072, 073, 074, 076, 077, 077A. Spokeshaves: A51, A51R, A151, A151R

<u>November 1933 – Catalogue No 12 and 12A of 1934</u>
Plough Planes: 050A, 405 and extra bases for 405

<u>Small undated publicity catalogue issued between January 1934 Price List and November 1935 Catalogue No 14</u>
Block Planes: 09½, 015, 016, 017, 018, 019.
Rebate Planes: 041, 042. Plough Planes: 043, 044

<u>November 1935 – Catalogue No 14</u>
Block Planes: 0101. Rebate Planes: 311, 712, 713, 714, 1366, 2506, 2506S. Plough Planes: 040. Router: 722
Scrub Plane: 400½. Spokeshaves: 052, 052R, 0152, 0152R

<u>December 1936 – Small publicity catalogue</u>
Spokeshaves: A63, A64

<u>February 1938 – Catalogue No 15</u>
Block Planes: 0100, 0100½

March 1939 – Dated publicity leaflet
Bench Plane: T5

June 1954 – Price List
Chamfershave: A65

1955 – Pocket catalogue No 16
Fibreboard Planes: 730, 735

January 1959 – Price List
Rebate Plane: 778

1970 – Price List
Plough Planes: 044C, 050C

October 1982 – Catalogue
Block Plane: 060½. Plough Plane: 045C

October 1988 - Catalogue
Bench Plane: CS88

January 1992 - Catalogue
Bench Plane: SP4

1995 - Catalogue
Bench Plane: SP5

Edward Preston Planes

Planes added to the range in catalogues No 12 and No 14 included models which were originally patented and produced by Edward Preston and Sons Ltd. the Birmingham rule, level and plane manufacturer. Preston's had fallen into financial difficulties in the early 1930's that resulted in them being absorbed by John Rabone and Sons Ltd, their main competitor, in October 1932.

Subsequent to the takeover, Rabone's made an attempt to re-organise the iron plane making section at Preston's Whittall Works but after two years arrived at the decision that "Certain products were found not to conform readily with the company's (Rabone's) other interests." John Rabone therefore felt it necessary to dispose of the manufacturing rights which they eventually did to C & J Hampton on 1 October 1934. The products included iron planes and spokeshaves, brass plumb bobs and beech mitre boxes.

However an August 1933 price list of Record's includes the following planes which were previously manufactured by Edward Preston:

Shoulder Rebates (improved): 072, 073, 074
Bullnose Rebate: 076, 077, 077A

A further seven iron planes of Preston design were eventually included in the Record range to which the No 1405 brass plumb bob and No 568 beech mitre box were also added.

John Rabone inherited the stock of Preston planes which they catalogued in some editions of their 1934 catalogue No 27. Sub-section pages 1A to 10A at the back of this catalogue are dedicated to Preston metal planes and other products. Rabones were left to dispose of this stock through their own outlets. Some Preston bench planes, produced under John Rabone management, have a Rabone transfer affixed to the handle spur.

All the Record planes of Edward Preston design are listed below with the original Preston pattern number in brackets:

Shoulder Rebate: 041 (1368)
Shoulder Rebate: 042 (1368A)
Shoulder Rebate: 072 (1368B)
Shoulder Rebate: 073 (1368C)
Shoulder Rebate: 074 (1368D)
Bullnose Rebate: 076 (1366)
Bullnose Rebate: 077 (1355)
Bullnose Rebate: 077A (2509)
3 in 1 Plane: 311 (311)
BullnoseRebate:076(1363)
Side Rebate: 2506 (2506)
Side Rebate: 2506S (2506S)
Router: (22)

As can be seen the only planes to retain their original Preston pattern numbers were the 311, 2506 and 2506S.

Production Periods for Planes

The range of planes produced was greatest between 1938 and 1940 when the No 15 catalogue, reproduced in this volume, showed 58 different planes and 18 spokeshaves. However the intervention of WW2 caused many of the patterns to be listed as "temporarily out of production," as seen in the 1 May 1943 price list. Wartime restrictions had by April 1941 caused production of hand drills, plumb bobs, jacks and selected vices to stop. No doubt the company hoped to resume production of the full product line after hostilities had ceased.

Some of the withdrawn planes were still listed in various editions of the No 16 pocket catalogue throughout the 1950's up to the 1962 edition. However no spare parts were listed for them in the 'parts' section of the catalogues from 1953 onwards nor did they appear on separate price lists after the revised one of January 1948. This suggests that they were not returned to production. The subsequent No 17 catalogue of 1963 displayed a much reduced range of planes but one which probably still met the requirements of the 1960's woodworker.

The lists which follow identify the planes that were withdrawn and those that were re-introduced after the war.

Planes Out of Production from around 1943 but in the catalogue until 1952
02: Smoother. 052: Spokeshave. 077: Bullnose Rebate. 052R: Spokeshave. 1366: Bullnose Rebate. 053: Spokeshave. 400½: Scrub. 055: Spokeshave. 0100: Block. 063: Spokeshave. 0100½: Block. 064: Spokeshave. 0101: Block. 0152: Spokeshave. 0152R: Spokeshave.

Planes Out of Production from around 1943 but in the catalogue until 1962
072: Shoulder Rebate. 015: Block. 074: Shoulder Rebate. 016: Block. 712: Skew Rebate. 017: Block. 713: Skew Rebate. 019: Block. 714: Skew Rebate. 0230: Block. 040: Plough. 0113: Circular. 071½: Router.

Planes Re-introduced from 1943
The following patterns were listed as out of production in 1943 but whilst still appearing in catalogues they did not appear in price lists until the dates shown below. Their inclusion in catalogue No 17 of 1963, and its related price lists, confirms their re-introduction to the product line.

Corrugated bases to bench planes – prices on application from 1949 onwards. T5: Technical Jack from 1952 onwards. 041: Shoulder Rebate from 1953 onwards. 2506: Side Rebate from 1953 onwards 2506S: Side Rebate from 1953 onwards. 722: Router from 1953 onwards. 405: Hollow and Round extra bases from 1953 onwards. 018: Block from 1959 onwards.

All other pattern numbers not listed above enjoyed continuous production through to the late 1960's.

New Planes Introduced after 1954
A65: Chamfershave 1954. 050C: Plough Plane 1972. 730: Fibreboard Plane 1955. 045C: Plough Plane 1982. 735: Fibreboard Plane 1955. 060½ Block Plane 1982. 778 Rebate Plane 1959. CS88: Bench Plane 1988. 044C: Plough Plane 1971. SP4: Bench Plane 1992. SP5: Bench Plane 1995

A65 Chamfershave: - A late addition to the spokeshave range and with a very short production life of around 10 years. It was provided with two angled adjustable fences on the sole that allowed various widths of chamfers to be worked uniformly.

730 Fibreboard Plane: - Introduced to allow slitting and bevelling of soft insulating board by the use of thin razor-blade type cutters which were provided in cartons of 6. Two cutter positions were provided: a vertical position for slitting and a 45° angled position for bevelling. An attachable fence was provided for bevelling work. It remained in production for about 15 years.

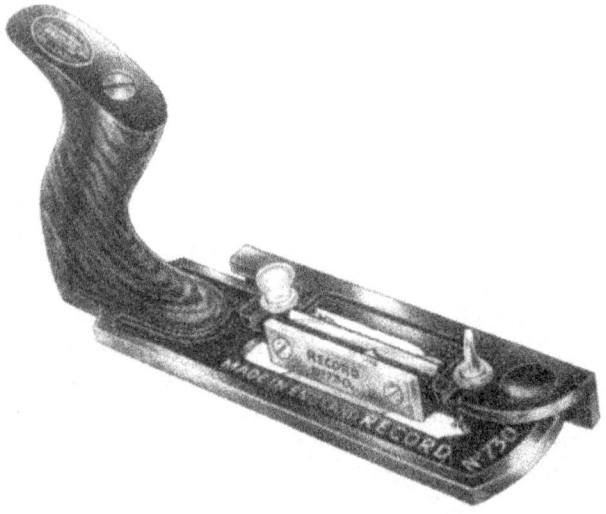

735 Fibreboard Plane: - Similar uses to the No 730 but in addition could also bevel hardboard using the thicker cutter provided with the attachable fence. A front knob was also fitted for extra stability when working the denser hardboard. A separate grooving attachment was also included to allow vee grooving of softboard, for decorative purposes, using the razor blade cutters. The plane survived in production into the early 1980's.

044C Plough Plane: - Introduced as "an entirely new design that supersedes the No 044 plough plane". Ten cutters were provided in a plastic wallet of which 7 were imperial sizes and 4 were metric. A new design of depth stop incorporated a nylon expander for positive locking. A handle made from cellulose acetate was screwed to the rear of the planes body casting. The plane survived in production into the early 1980's.

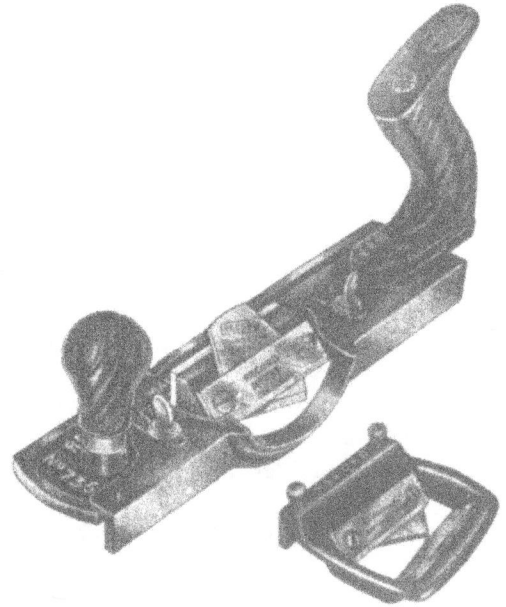

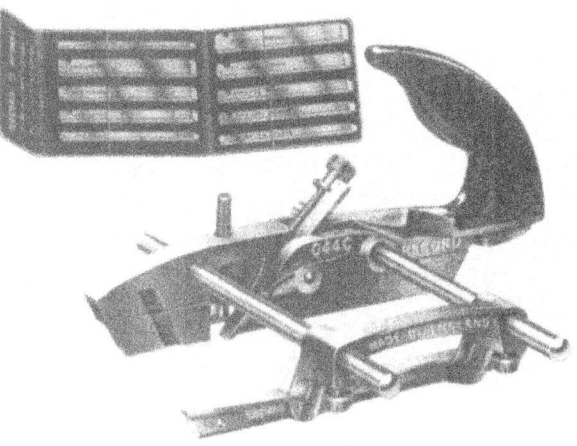

778 Rebate Plane: - This plane was produced by C & J Hampton from 1959 as a result of their acquisition of the Woden tool brand which was owned by The Steel Nut & Joseph Hampton Ltd. Woden Tools were based at Wednesbury in Staffordshire and, alongside their other products, manufactured a small range of woodworking planes which they originally acquired from W.S. Tools, a company based in Birmingham. The 778 was manufactured in addition to the No 078 duplex rebate plane, of similar design, but had the improvement of a screw adjustable cutter and two fence arms. The plane is still in production.

050C Combination Plane: - This plane was also introduced as "completely new and supersedes the No 050 combination plough plane". Eighteen cutters were provided as standard: 12 plough cutters of which 4 were metric, 5 beading cutters and 1 tonguing cutter. A new design of spur was attached to the front end of the plane body and the sliding section for cross-grain work as on the planing of housings. The depth stop and handle were the same as on the 044C.

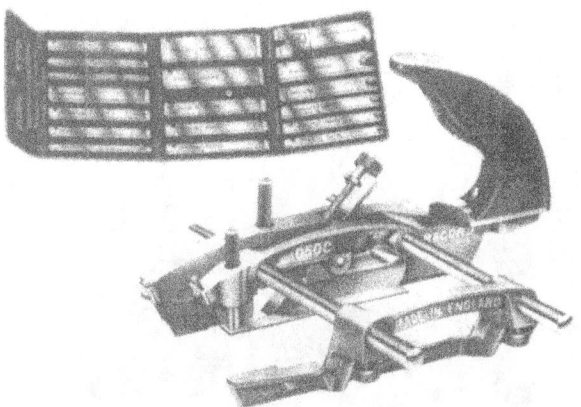

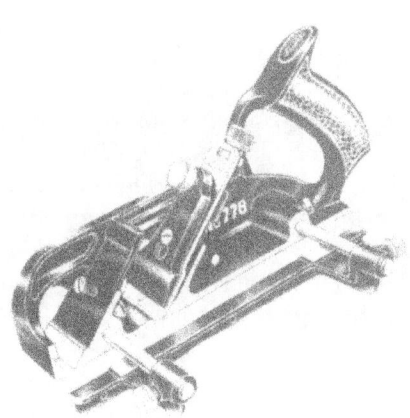

045C Plough Plane: - This plane was of similar design to the 044C and 050C which both preceded it. It was sold as a basic plough plane with only one cutter of 4mm width provided. If purchasers needed other widths of cutter these could be obtained up to ½" wide either individually or as a walleted set of 9. To

vii

allow the plane to undertake the work of a combination plough plane a conversion kit was offered, No K050C, which permitted a further 8 cutters to be used. These extra cutters consisted of 2 plough cutters, 5 beading cutters and 1 tonguing cutter. These cutters could also be obtained individually or as a set in a plastic wallet. This arrangement allowed purchasers to build up a set of cutters which were best suited to their needs.

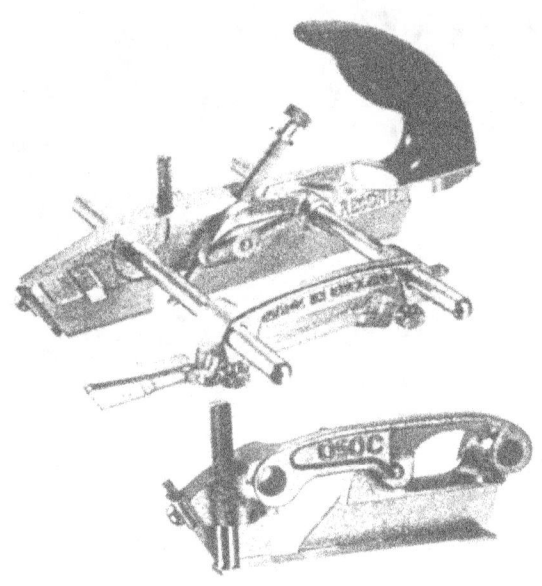

0601/2 Block Plane: - This was Record's first conventional block plane to have a very low cutter angle of 12½° instead of the normal 20° pitch. This low cutter angle required an in-line direct acting cutter adjustment wheel. At 6" in length it is equipped with an adjustable mouth but no lateral adjustment lever is provided. The cutter width is 15/8". On its introduction the lever cap was fitted with a cam lever to secure the cutter but since 1995 this has been replaced with a large brass screw. The names Record and Marples appear on the body casting either side of the front knob.

CS88 Smoothing Plane: - This had the shortest production period of any Record plane, as it was introduced in the 1988 catalogue and last listed in the October 1990 one. Developed by production engineer Martin Calvert and plane production manager Mel Stevens, and often referred to as the Calvert-Stevens, the plane incorporated several innovations of previous years and was meant to fill the gap left by Norris planes. The heavy body casting was fitted with an accurately machined frog seating which limited lateral movement of the frog as it was adjusted to open or close the plane mouth. Forward and backward movement of the frog was achieved with a large knurled brass adjustment screw.

Cutter adjustment was by a Norris type mechanism that controlled the depth of cut and lateral movement together. The laminated steel cutter, which was made in Japan, was fitted with a stay set cap iron and the whole secured on the frog with a gunmetal lever cap and a large knurled brass lever cap screw.

A rosewood handle and knob were fitted. Each plane was individually marked with a production number on the body casting underneath the rear of the handle. The body and frog were enamelled dark green and the plane was supplied in a baize-lined wooden box.

SP4 Smoothing Plane: - An economy version of the No 04 smoothing plane. Originally furnished with a handle and knob made of beech finished with clear lacquer but current production models have plastic ones fitted. The lever cap is painted blue and fitted with a large brass securing screw in line with the rest of the current bench plane range. The names Record and Marples appear on the body casting around the knob. There is no frog adjustment screw fitted.

SP5 Jack Plane: - This plane is of similar design to the No SP4 but is of jack plane length.

Discontinued Planes after 1963
The majority of planes in production at the time of catalogue No 17 survived to about 1972. However with the gradual introduction of power tools into the woodworking industries it was perhaps inevitable that certain specialised planes, for which demand had reduced, would be discontinued. The reduction in pattern numbers continued through the 1970's to the current date but a few new planes were introduced.

The last catalogue listings of planes before they became discontinued are detailed below:

1963 to 1965
Chamfershave: A65
Stay-set cap irons for bench planes discontinued

1967
Block Plane: 018
Rebate Planes: 010½, 041, 075, 2506
Spokeshaves: A51, A51R, 051, 051R, 0151, 0151R

1970
Plough Planes: 044, 050
Fibreboard Plane: 730

1971
Router: 722
Corrugated bases for bench plane: 04½, 05½, 08 discontinued

1972 to 1980
Bench Plane: T5. Block Plane: 0102. Rebate Planes: 078, 042, 076, 2506S. Plough Planes: 043, 050C. Scraper Planes: 070, 080. Fibreboard Plane - 735 Spokeshaves - A63, A64. Router - 071. Extra hollow and round bases for 405 Multiplane

1982
Bench Plane - 08. Block Planes - 0120, 0130. Rebate Plane - 311 but was re-introduced briefly in 1987. Plough Planes - 405, 044C

1990
Bench Plane - CS88

1993
Corrugated bases discontinued as an option on the remaining bench plane production

1994
Bench Plane - 06. Block Planes - 0110, 0220. Rebate Planes - 311, 077, 073, 010

1995
Plough Plane - 045C

1996
Bench Planes - 04½, 05½

1997
Bench Plane - 03

In Production in 2001
Bench Planes - SP4, SP5, 04, 05, 07. Block Planes - 060½, 09½. Rebate Plane - 778. Circular Plane - 020C. Spokeshaves - A151, A151R
The 04 smooth plane, 05 jack plane and the 07 jointer plane have the distinction of attaining the longest period of continuous production from the original plane line of 1931, a total of over 70 years.

Patents

Most of the patents filed by C & J Hampton related to tools other than planes. Their entrance into the woodworking plane market involved manufacturing a proven range of planes for which any patents had long expired. However on the introduction of the first Record planes, in January 1931, an application for patent No. 362743 was made which was subsequently granted on 10 December 1931. This patent related to a two piece cap iron called a stay set. At that time English patents lasted 16 years so the invention was protected from infringement until December 1947. All stay set cap irons made during this period were marked with the patent number, but after 1947 protection ceased so subsequently cap irons were not marked until they were eventually deleted from the range in the mid 1960's.

Record bench planes could be bought with the stay set cap iron as original equipment instead of the standard cap iron at no extra cost to the purchaser. Planes so equipped at the works had a lever cap with "SS" cast into it above the lever cap screw hole. The box label also had "SS" after the plane model number. Stay set cap irons bought separately as a spare part were more expensive than the standard cap iron. Planes offered with the stay set cap iron as an option were the bench planes Nos 02 through to No 08 and the technical jack plane No T5.

The patent specification drawings are reproduced on the next page. Curiously they do not show the cap iron as it was finally produced. The stay set cap iron as it was actually produced is shown below:

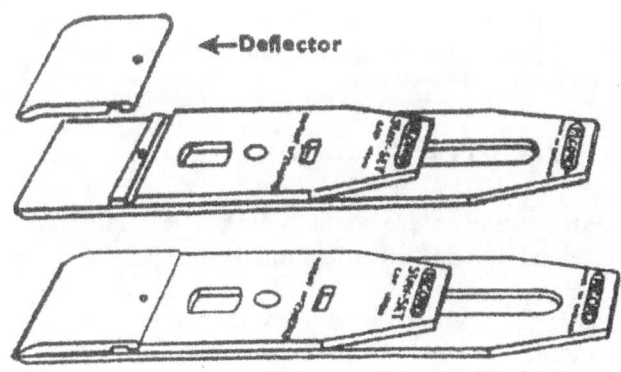

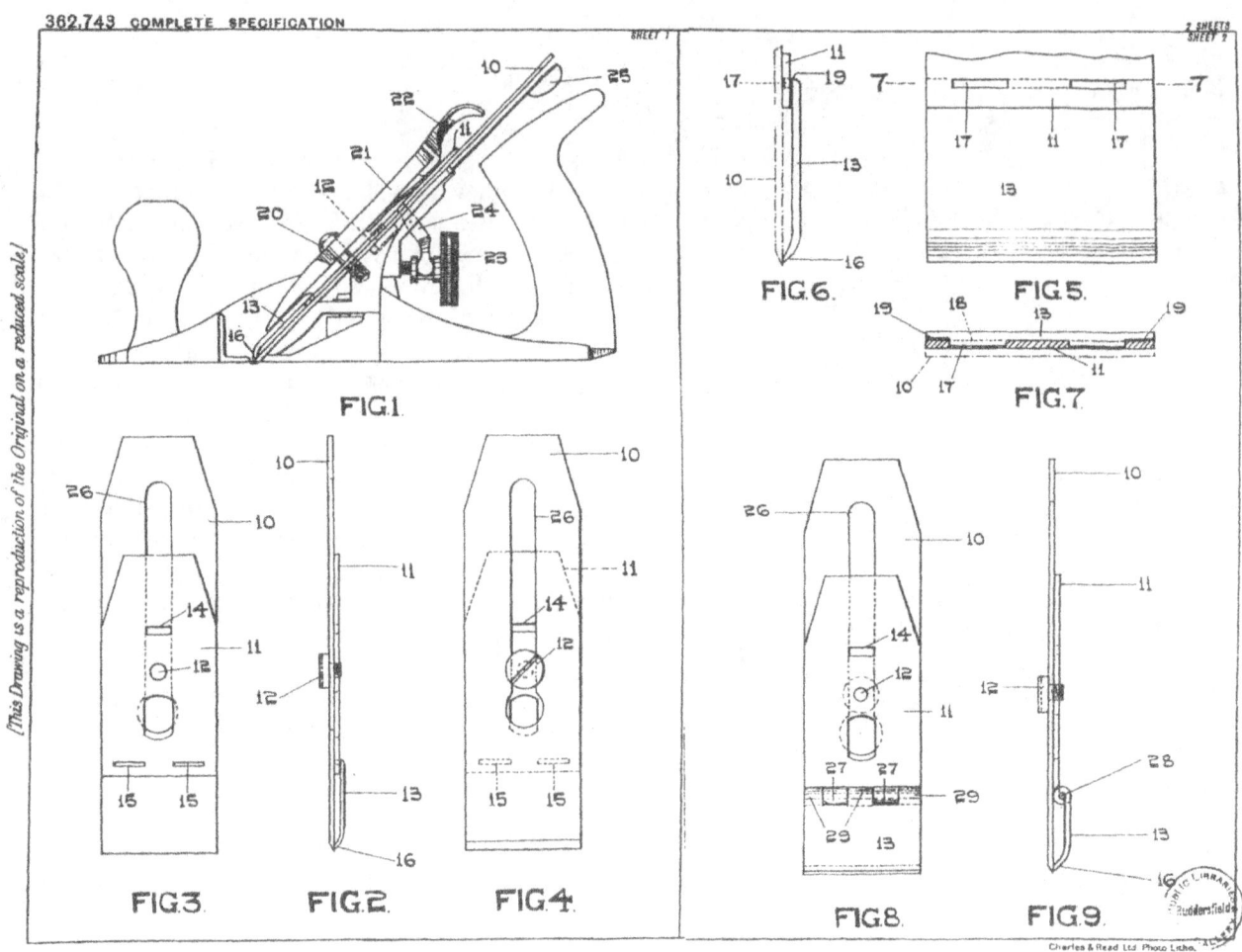

The only other plane-related patents were numbered as follows and granted on the date indicated:

Fibreboard Planes: 730 (741796, 14 Dec 1955), 730, 735 (755582, 22 Aug 1956), 735 (757574, 19 Sept 1956)

These patents concerned the clamping of the cutters in the planes, and their attachments, for working fibreboard and hardboard.

Registered Designs

Only two types of planes designed by C & J Hampton received a registered design number.

Three skew rebate planes were numbered 712, 713 and 714 and were 1¼", 1½" and 1¾" wide respectively. The design was first registered on 12 November 1935 and first marketed in No 14 catalogue in November 1935. Registered designs had a duration of 5 years after which copyright could be extended for 5 year periods up to a maximum of 15 years. The copyright protection on this design expired on 12 November 1950. During the copyright period the plane had the mark REGD. DESIGN No 807853 appearing on the lower right-hand side of the body casting near the sole. The skew rebate was listed as withdrawn in 1943, but examples exist without the design number marked on them.

A plough plane, numbered 044, also first appeared in the November 1935 catalogue No 14 but did not become registered until 30 March 1936. Copyright protection was also extended on this plane for the full 15 years until final expiry on 30 March 1951. The plane had the mark REGD. DESIGN No 811133, appearing on the rear left-hand side of the skate for about 15 years only.

Dating Planes

The age of a particular model of plane can be established by studying various aspects of its construction details and its original packaging, if available. Parts on planes were very often interchanged or replaced, due to wear or breakages, so cutters and handles are not totally reliable to establish age. Short production periods can date models such as the 0100 and 0100½ block planes with reasonable accuracy, as both had only been in production about 5 years before wartime restrictions caused them to be withdrawn.

However various other methods can be used to date models which had longer production runs, and the following information will provide a guide for when a particular model was manufactured.

Modifications and Additions to Planes
Planes not listed below remained essentially unchanged during their production lives.

02 to 08 Bench Planes
Plane Body
• A corrugated sole became available as an optional extra in 1932.
• The curved top edge to the sides and the curved toe and heel of the body casting had a ground finish until about 1955 to 1960. They were subsequently left as cast and enamelled blue.
• The frog receiver in the body casting was modified from a straight central rib to a wishbone shaped buttress around 1955 to 1960.
• Plane numbers 06, 07 and 08 had a central strengthening rib added to the body casting from 1963 onwards.

Frog Assembly
• War-time production had "War Finish" marked on the lateral lever.
• The frog design was changed from having straight sides and a flat machined cutter seating to ogee-shaped sides and a recessed surface to the cutter seating from 1957.
• The revolving disc on the lower end of the lateral lever was provided until WW2. Thereafter a solid disc was fitted until the introduction of a one piece pressed steel lever.
• The Y lever, which engages the cutter and cap iron assembly for cutter adjustment, changed from a one piece iron casting to a two piece pressed steel component in the late 1960's.
• A modification to the frog adjusting mechanism saw a milled slot introduced on the rear underside of the frog casting to accommodate the redesigned frog adjusting screw from August 1976. This replaced the previously used captive head adjusting screw and fork.
• A lateral lever made of one piece pressed steel replaced the previously used three piece fabricated lever from around 1985.

Cutter and Cap Iron
• The cutter and cap iron on the 05½ jack plane was changed from 2¼" in width to 2 3/8" wide around 1937 to 1938 to match the cutter width with 04½, 06 and 07 bench planes.
• The profile of the cutter and cap iron changed from a straight top with angled corners to a curved top with angled corners from about 1956 to 1959.

Lever Cap
• Metal plating to the lever cap and small screws was nickel until WW2 when plating was discontinued during war production. An alternative plating was applied during the immediate post-war years before chromium plating became standard about 1956.
• A knurled brass screw to secure the lever cap replaced the cam lever from 1995 onwards.

Handle and Knob
• Rosewood was used for the handle and knob until WW2. Post-war production used dark stained beech until 1998.
• Impact resistant resin (plastic) replaced wood for the handles and knobs from 1998 onwards.

T5 Technical Jack: - A prototype of this model exists with No 05¼ on the body casting but with no side handle provided or tapping to receive a handle in the body casting. This model number never appeared in any catalogues and it was redesignated number T5 for its March 1939 introduction to the market. Originally equipped with a 2¼" cutting iron prior to its WW2 suspension but altered to a 2" iron on its post-war re-introduction in 1952. The plane did not appear in catalogues until 1952 and early publicity leaflets aimed it at schools and technical colleges. A locknut for the brass cutter adjusting wheel was offered as an option to prevent unnecessary adjustment by pupils in school workshops. The plane survived until the 1970's.

010 and 010½ Bench Rebate Planes: - These had similar changes to 02 to 08 bench planes. In addition hardened steel spurs were offered as an optional extra in the 1949 catalogue for cross-grain work but there is no evidence in the price lists to suggest that this option went into long term production. However examples are known to exist with the spurs on them.

For either of these planes to be obtained with the optional spurs they had to be specified as 010S and 010½S when ordering. The plane was always equipped with an adjustable frog, as on the bench planes, which is how they differ from their Stanley equivalent that never had a frog adjusting screw.

043 Plough Plane: - Originally a plane with a single arm fence when it first appeared around early 1935.

It was soon modified to a double arm bridged fence and with a wider flared palm rest. It may have been modified to permit the introduction of the 040 plough in November 1935 at a lower price. The flat depth stop and fence arm thumb screws were changed to a round screw with a knurled edge around the late 1950's. Metric cutters were stated as optional extras in widths of 4, 6, 9 and 12 mm from 1935. It seems strange that a plough designed for the light duty use of cutting up to ¼" wide grooves should have the option of metric cutters up to 12mm wide offered. At that time no other manufacturer produced a plough like this, so this could well be Record's own design.

044 Plough: - (See also Registered Designs) Early models were not provided with a cutter adjusting-screw or a bridged fence, both of which first appeared in catalogue No 14 of November 1935.

The plane was provided with a pair of long and short fence arms from November 1935 onwards. Metric cutters were offered as optional extras in widths of 4, 6, 9 and 12 mm from 1935. The additional cutter cramping screw, which was provided to stop lateral movement of the cutter, was added in 1949. The depth stop screw and fence arm screws were also changed to match the 043's around the late 1950's. Cutters for this did not fit any other model number of Record plough planes.

050 and 050A Ploughs: - On introduction the 050 lacked the cutter adjusting wheel which was added in November 1933. A bridged fence was provided about 1935.

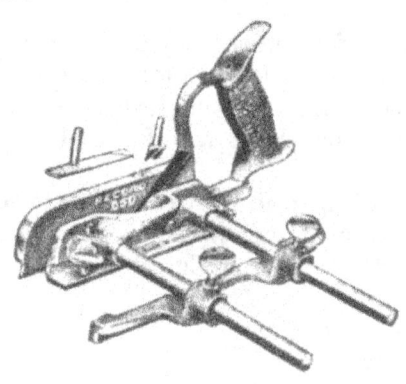

From its introduction in November 1933 the 050A was produced alongside the 050 as an option until about 1943, when the 050 was deleted and the 050A became the standard. Metric cutters were offered as optional extras in widths of 4, 6, 9 and 12 mm from 1935. The fence arms had threaded ends to screw into the body casting up to about the mid 1950's. Thereafter plain fence arms were used and secured with a screw in the body casting. Cutters for this did not fit any other model number of Record plough plane.

071 and 071½ Routers: - The only addition to these models was the adjustable sole fence that allowed the router to cut grooves parallel to the edge of the work. The fence first appears in the November 1933 catalogue. Earlier models were not provided with fence grooves on the sole or threaded screw attachment holes for the fence.

080 Scraper: - Fine and coarse toothing cutters were offered as options from 1933 onwards.

076, 077 and 077A Bullnose Rebates: - Early examples of these planes had a small triangular shaped panel recess on each side of the plane which had a chequered pattern cast in it. However this feature does not appear in any catalogue photographs which always show the planes with flat machined sides. Later models appear as depicted in the catalogues. Early 076 lever caps had RECORD BRITISH cast in the top and highlighted in orange paint on the blue enamel. The 077 and 077A had the same words high-cast into the top of the lever cap. In 1969 the lever cap of the 076 and 077A had been redesigned with a more modern profile and no name cast into it.

311 Bullnose and Shoulder Rebate: - Early models had a similar triangular shaped design to the 076, 077 and 077A. In addition when the shoulder nose section was attached the appearance of the plane was of a low and graceful shape whereas later models, of 1950's onwards, had a heavier casting with the plane looking distinctly taller with the shoulder section attached. Early lever caps had the words RECORD BRITISH cast in the top and highlighted in blue paint. Later models just had RECORD cast into the top of the lever cap. WW2 production had "War finish" marked on the side of the body casting. The lever cap was also modified in later years as the 076 and 077A.

712, 713 and 714 Skew Rebates: - (See also Registered Designs) Late production examples without the design number mark may be found without a depth stop or provision to attach one onto the body casting. On these examples a small chequered panel design replaces the usual machined groove provided for locating a depth stop.

Wood Fittings

Prior to the early 1950's all bench plane handles and knobs, block plane and side rebate knobs, and the cutting iron wedge on the 1366 were listed as selected rosewood. Thereafter they were listed as from selected hardwood which was usually beech lacquered dark brown. However in practice it is likely that beech was used from the beginning of WW2 onwards as rosewood became difficult to obtain.

The 405 retained rosewood fittings until 1962 when it to began to use selected hardwood.

The 400½ scrub plane, 071 and 071½ routers always had beech handles and knobs.

Throughout its production period of nearly 40 years the 070 box scraper had a clear finished ash handle.

Metal Plating

Certain model numbers were listed as being fully nickel plated on their introduction in catalogue No 12 of 1933. These were Plough: 050, Multiplane: 405. Bullnose Rebate: 77 & 77A. Shoulder Rebates: 72, 073, 074.

However in 1935 the No 14 catalogue listed all the above planes as being "Rustless plated" along with the following newly introduced models: Bullnose Shoulder Rebate: 311. Shoulder Rebates: 041, 042. Side Rebates: 2506, 2506S. Bullnose Rebate: 1366. Ploughs: 043, 044, 050A

Examples produced in this period can be observed with a dull grey metal coating that may be cadmium plating.

Catalogue No 15 of 1938 lists the planes as nickel plated with the exception of the 050, 050A and 405, which remained rustless plated.

The onset of WW2 caused government restrictions to be imposed on the use of nickel for non-essential purposes. This, coupled with a much reduced wartime product range, resulted in a ground and lacquered finish to the 042, 073, 077A and 311 rebate planes. They were also stamped 'War finish' on the body casting. Later models of these were never plated. Bench plane lever caps and small screws were also furnished unplated during the war.

Whilst nickel restrictions were in force the plough planes were plated with a nickel alternative along with the side rebates which made a post-war reappearance.

All planes which previously had had nickel plating on them carried a "Ministry of Supply Restriction" label, dated 1951, affixed to the lid of their boxes to confirm that an alternative plating had been applied, although the box labels still identified the contents as 'nickel plated'.

> (RECORD)
> The Ministry of Supply Order 1951 No. 1048 prohibits the use of Nickel Plating on Planes, and an alternative Metal Plating is now used.

Chromium plating appeared on bench plane lever caps from 1956 and the 018 block plane's knuckle joint lever cap and fittings from its re-introduction in 1959.

The last No 16 catalogue in 1962 listed the 2506, 2506S, 043, 044, 050 and 405 as plated.

Cutter Markings

All plane cutters were marked Record. The bench and block plane cutters were additionally marked Best

Crucible Cast Tungsten Steel up to around 1960.

Thereafter Tungsten Vanadium Steel was marked on them. Most of the other planes in the range had the Record and Tungsten Steel mark applied unless the iron was very small, in which case the mark was only Record.

Trade Label

C & J Hampton registered the Record trademark in 1909 and the products were better recognised by the name Record than that of the manufacturers C & J Hampton and subsequent owners. The trademark was incorporated into an oval, as shown below, and applied in various sizes by water-slide transfer to most of the product range. The lettering and border were in gold on a blue background. After 1960 the blue background became transparent.

Paint Colour

The planes with a painted finish were advertised in catalogues as Record Blue but the shade did vary over the years. The spokeshaves which had their numbers prefixed by **A** were made of malleable iron and painted red. Cellulose paint was used pre WW2 and subsequently stove enamel. The name Record on bench plane lever caps was highlighted in orange throughout most of the production years but was omitted from the early 1990's. Early block planes prior to WW2 also had Record highlighted in orange on the lever caps.

Packaging

The type of box which a plane is supplied in can be an indication of its age. With a few exceptions, which are dealt with separately, Record planes were supplied in boxes as follows:

Pre-WW2: - Dark blue paper-covered strawboard box with the contents labels on each end of the lid. Very early large planes may be seen with the box contents label on one end and a side of the lid.

WW2 to 1962: - Lighter blue paper-covered strawboard or card box with contents label on one end only. Until 1962 the box contents label had a blue and white border surrounding a yellow background with the contents stated.

1962 to 1970's: - A straw coloured paper covered card box with a blue and yellow contents label on one end.

1970's to 1980's: - A blue and white printed box made of corrugated cardboard. Until 1972 the box was marked C & J Hampton Ltd and then until 1982 Record Ridgway Tools Ltd.

Current: - The 04 and 05 bench planes, 778 rebate plane and 020C circular plane are furnished in a cardboard carton with their respective pictures, and description, printed on it. The 07 jointer plane is provided with a plain brown cardboard carton and the SP4 and SP5 bench planes, 060½ and 09½ block planes and the A151 spokeshaves are marketed in a card backed blister pack for sales display purposes.

Packaging Exceptions: -Up to about 1945 to 1950 the following model numbers were furnished in a clear varnished wooden box with a sliding lid which was labelled on the end: Shoulder Rebates: 041, 042, 072, 073, 074. Bullnose Rebate: 077, 077A. 3 in 1 Rebate Plane: 311. Plough Plane: 050

The 405 Multiplane was always shown in the catalogues in a clear varnished wooden box with a hinged lid that was offered as follows: <u>Pre-war</u>: Wide and low box with cutters housed in a rack in one end of it. <u>Post-war</u>: Tall and narrow box with cutters contained in a separate removable holding rack.

The 044 Plough and 050 Combination planes were offered from about 1950 to early 1960's in dark blue leatherette paper covered cardboard boxes with hinged lids. From then to the end of manufacture a straw coloured cardbox with a lid was provided. A few examples of the 405 have been found packaged in this way. These may be WW2 production when restrictions applied to the use of timber.

Over the years Record absorbed other companies whose products were added to the tools produced. These companies included Woden, who had a similar product line to Record; Gilbow, who contributed tin snips, shears and cold chisels to the range and Marples, renowned for their woodworking tools, and Ridgway, who added wood boring tools to the range.

Whilst it is sad to see that the company's current production of planes is much reduced from the extent of its earlier years, it still offers the woodworking industry quality hand tools that satisfy the demands of woodworkers for the 21st century. It is to be hoped that Record will continue as a name to be recognised in the manufacture of high quality tools for many more years to come.

The Catalogue

This volume contains a reprint of an original Catalogue No 15 of 1938 that, unusually, was undated. After the catalogue's initial printing, a loose sheet numbered 42A was inserted showing the modelmakers' block planes that were also available. This insert appears on the next page of this book.

Acknowledgements

I would like to express my gratitude to Record Tools for their kind permission to reprint this 1938 catalogue as well as the other illustrations throughout the Introduction.

Thanks are extended to The Patent Office for permission to reprint the original specification drawings on page x. Special thanks go also to The Hawley Collection Trust at Sheffield University, who have very kindly allowed me to research their extensive archives on the history of C & J Hampton and Record Tools, to Ken Hawley for his help and guidance, to Cav Shaw, whose advice was very helpful during my early collecting days, and to Roy Arnold, whose original encouragement for me to document the Record plane has resulted in this publication.

Leslie Harrison   March 2003

Catalogue No. 15, Page 42A

C. & J. HAMPTON, LTD.   -   -   MANUFACTURERS

RECORD MODEL MAKERS' PLANE
No. 0100½.
With TUNGSTEN STEEL Cutting Iron.

No. 0100½ Model Makers' Plane is non-adjustable. It is suitable for Model Makers, Violin and Pattern Makers, etc.

The Base is convex both on the width and length, $\frac{7}{8}''$ radius on the width and 12" radius on the length.

The Cutter is tightened in position by a knurled screw.

$3\frac{1}{2}''$ long.   1" Cutter.   Weight ½ pound.

Code Word : Irger.

PRICE ... **4/9** each.

RECORD BLOCK PLANE
No. 0100.
With TUNGSTEN STEEL Cutting Iron.

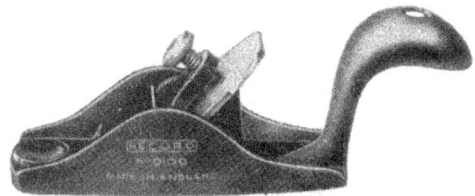

No. 0100 Block Plane is fitted with Iron Handle and is non-adjustable.

The Cutter is tightened in position by a knurled screw.

$3\frac{1}{2}''$ long.   1" Cutter.   Weight $\frac{3}{8}$ pound.

Code Word : Irgap.

PRICE ... **2/-** each.

All Planes packed 1 per box.

RECORD WORKS   -   -   SHEFFIELD, ENGLAND

RECORD TOOLS

C. & J. HAMPTON, LTD.
SHEFFIELD
ENGLAND

Catalogue No. 15.

Telegrams and Cables:
RECORD, SHEFFIELD

Telephones:
SHEFFIELD 41294
(4 lines)

Codes:
A.B.C. 5th and 6th Editions
Marconi International
Western Union
Bentley's

Copyright.   Printed in England.

RECORD WORKS, SHEFFIELD, ENGLAND.
Photographs of our two Factories taken from an aeroplane.

C. & J. HAMPTON, LTD.   -   -   MANUFACTURERS

FOREWORD

IN presenting this No. 15 Catalogue of Record Tools manufactured by us at Record Works, Sheffield, England, we call attention to the many new lines which have been added to the range of Record Tools during the past few years.

Our two Factories are of modern design and lay-out, and are equipped with up-to-date plant for the specialised production of Record Tools.

The design, material and performance of Record Tools are always under close scrutiny and where improvements are found necessary to meet modern conditions our experience and facilities enable us to introduce new features to meet these demands.

Every tool is subjected to inspection not only during process of manufacture but finally before leaving the Factory to ensure that it is in every way correct.

It is our aim to make the line of Record Tools complete for present-day requirements of Users, and comprehensive to facilitate distribution and service through trade channels.

TO MERCHANTS AND DEALERS.
Only bona-fide Merchants and Dealers who carry stock for distribution are allowed Trade discounts, and in the general interests of the trade certain conditions are imposed to stabilise retail prices of Record Tools, so as to minimise price variation and bring about a consistency in selling prices.

TO CRAFTSMEN AND USERS.
We pledge ourselves to give satisfaction in regard to Record Tools and prompt service in the supply of Spares and Repairs.

We are always pleased to receive suggestions from Craftsmen and Users of Tools, and are prepared to offer our advice to those who are interested in products such as are manufactured by us.

Our facilities for testing any Tool or mechanical principle are at the disposal of designers and we welcome direct communications which contribute to the advancement of knowledge relating to Tools.

C. & J. Hampton, Ltd.

RECORD WORKS   -   -   SHEFFIELD, ENGLAND

C. & J. HAMPTON, LTD. - - MANUFACTURERS

GENERAL INFORMATION

MATERIALS: All the materials used in the manufacture of RECORD TOOLS are the best obtainable.

GUARANTEE: All RECORD TOOLS are guaranteed against defect in material or workmanship, and any part proving defective will be replaced free of charge, but no responsibility can be accepted for consequential damage or expenses.

ORDERS: Orders are accepted subject to the provision that deliveries may be wholly or partly suspended through delays caused by shortage of material or labour, strikes, failure of transport facilities, accidents or other happenings beyond our control.

COMPLAINTS: Every possible care and attention are given to the final examination and packing of all goods, but should there be any complaint please notify us at once.

INDENTING: When ordering or specifying Record Tools, please state the Article No. shown in the Catalogue, as this number identifies both article and size.

LITERATURE: Showcards and Leaflets are supplied to stockists of Record Tools to assist display and stimulate sales. Electrotypes will also be sent on request.

PATENTS and DESIGNS: All RECORD Patents and Designs are officially registered and protected in most countries, and our rights against infringement under these registrations will be enforced.

AGENCIES IN:

AUSTRALIA, CANADA, SOUTH AFRICA, BRITISH EAST AFRICA, NEW ZEALAND, INDIA, CHINA, SIAM, MALAY STATES, EAST INDIES, EGYPT, GREECE, ARGENTINE, BRAZIL, CHILE, MEXICO, WEST INDIES, NORWAY, SWEDEN, DENMARK, FINLAND, HOLLAND, FRANCE, BELGIUM, SWITZERLAND, SPAIN, PORTUGAL.

RECORD WORKS - - SHEFFIELD, ENGLAND

PLANES & SPOKE SHAVES
Pages 6-64

HAND & BREAST DRILLS
Pages 66-76

VICES for Metal and Wood
Pages 78-118

PIPE VICES WRENCHES & CUTTERS
Pages 120-134

BOLT CLIPPERS
Pages 136-142

CRAMPS
Pages 144-145

C. & J. HAMPTON, LTD.   -   -   MANUFACTURERS

RECORD ADJUSTABLE IRON PLANES

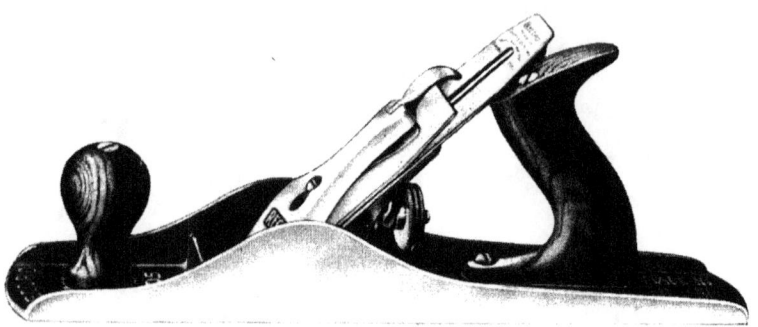

RECORD PLANES are made in a comprehensive range of patterns and sizes suitable for all purposes. They embody many notable improvements and are produced throughout with the greatest care and accuracy, which constitute guarantee of unsurpassed quality.

An outstanding feature in all Record Planes is the TUNGSTEN STEEL Cutting Iron, which is the outcome of research and tests which have been made with the object of producing a Steel which will retain its fine edge and fast cutting quality on the hardest woods.

This Cutting Iron is hardened and tempered under scientific control, which ensures accuracy and uniformity. It is precision-ground all over, and is tested and guaranteed to be the right temper.

The Lever Cap and all the small screws and parts are nickel-plated.

The Handle and Knob are made of genuine Rosewood, which is carefully selected for its beautiful colour and grain.

The Body is finished cellulose blue, and the base and sides are machine-ground and polished.

All parts are interchangeable, and Spare Irons and parts can be supplied.

RECORD WORKS   -   -   SHEFFIELD, ENGLAND

C. & J. HAMPTON, LTD. - - MANUFACTURERS

RECORD ADJUSTABLE IRON PLANES

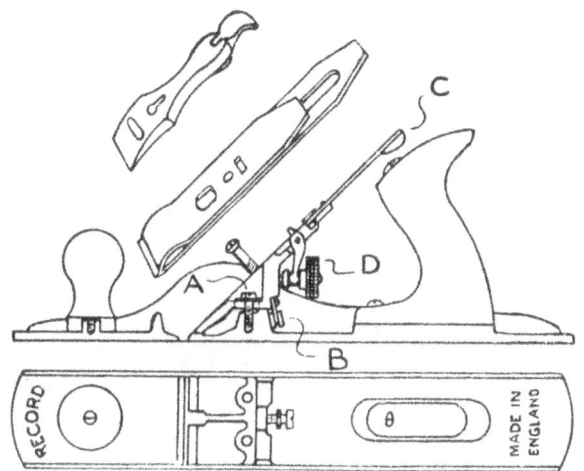

CONSTRUCTION.

The Body is made of high-grade Cast Iron of guaranteed strength, and is ribbed where necessary to ensure rigidity.

The illustration shows how the machined faces of the Frog bed firmly on to similar machined faces on the Body and are securely fastened in position by the two Frog Screws, which in effect makes the Frog solid with the Body and prevents chattering.

The Iron Cut Adjustment is accurately made to give very fine adjustment for cutting.

The Lateral Adjusting Lever is fitted with a turned Steel Roller for smooth working.

The genuine Rosewood Handle and Knob are fastened to the Body by Steel Studs with Brass Cap Nuts.

ADJUSTMENT.

1. The Cap Iron is, of course, adjustable on the Cutting Iron to give correct settings for fine or coarse cutting.
2. The width of the effective mouth, i.e., the distance from the Cutting Edge of the Iron to the forward edge of the mouth, can be regulated as required for fine or coarse cutting by loosening the two Frog Screws A (see sketch) and turning the Adjusting Screw B until the correct setting is obtained, and afterwards tightening the two Frog Screws A.
3. The Cutting Edge of the Iron can be adjusted parallel to the base of the Body by the Lateral Adjusting Lever C.
4. The depth of cut is adjusted by the Brass Nut D.

RECORD WORKS - - SHEFFIELD, ENGLAND

C. & J. HAMPTON, LTD.   -   -   MANUFACTURERS

RECORD ADJUSTABLE IRON PLANES

With Warranted Best Crucible Cast
TUNGSTEN STEEL Cutting Irons.

End and Side Adjustment of Cutters.
Handles and Knobs of Selected Rosewood.
Lever Caps and Small Screws Nickel Plated.

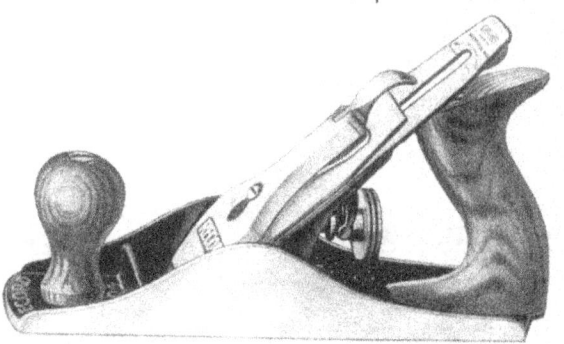

RECORD SMOOTH PLANES.

Plane No.	Type	Price each	Length Inches	Width of Cutter Inches	Weight Pounds	Code Word
02	Smooth	12/6	7¼	1⅝	2⅜	Ipaxo
03	Smooth	13/-	8	1¾	3¼	Ipbar
04	Smooth	13/6	9	2	3¾	Ipbes
04½	Smooth	16/-	10	2⅜	4¾	Ipbit

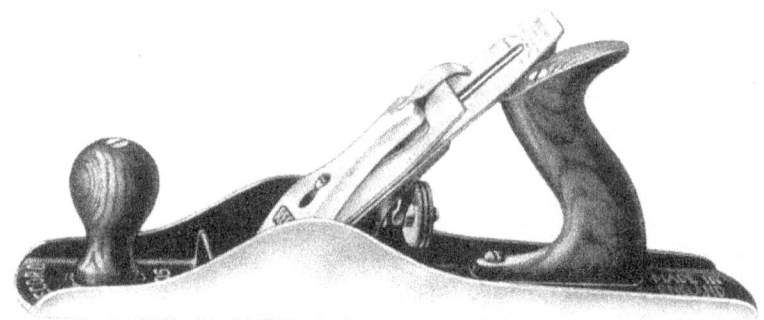

RECORD JACK PLANES.

Plane No.	Type	Price each	Length Inches	Width of Cutter Inches	Weight Pounds	Code Word
05	Jack	16/6	14	2	4¾	Ipblu
05½	Jack	18/6	15	2¼	6	Ipboy

Plane Irons and Plane Parts on pages 49 and 54.

All Planes packed 1 per box.

RECORD WORKS   -   -   SHEFFIELD, ENGLAND

C. & J. HAMPTON, LTD. - - MANUFACTURERS

RECORD ADJUSTABLE IRON PLANES

With Warranted Best Crucible Cast
TUNGSTEN STEEL Cutting Irons.

End and Side Adjustment of Cutters.
Handles and Knobs of Selected Rosewood.
Lever Caps and Small Screws Nickel Plated.

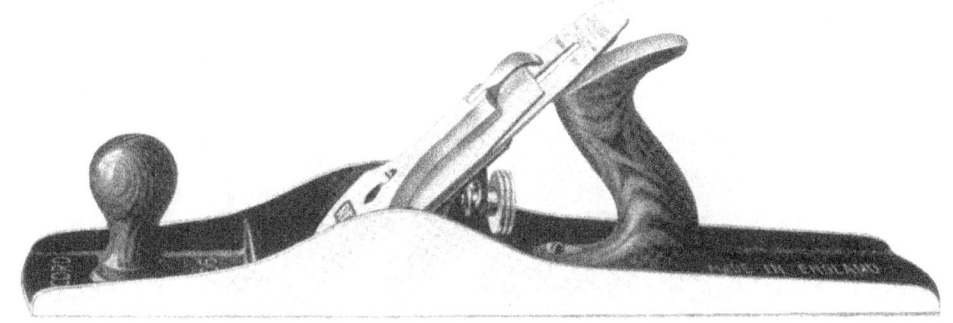

RECORD FORE AND JOINTER PLANES.

Plane No.	Type	Price each	Length Inches	Width of Cutter Inches	Weight Pounds	Code Word
06	Fore	21/–	18	$2\frac{3}{8}$	7	Ipcen
07	Jointer	25/–	22	$2\frac{3}{8}$	8	Ipcip
08	Jointer	30/–	24	$2\frac{5}{8}$	9	Ipcor

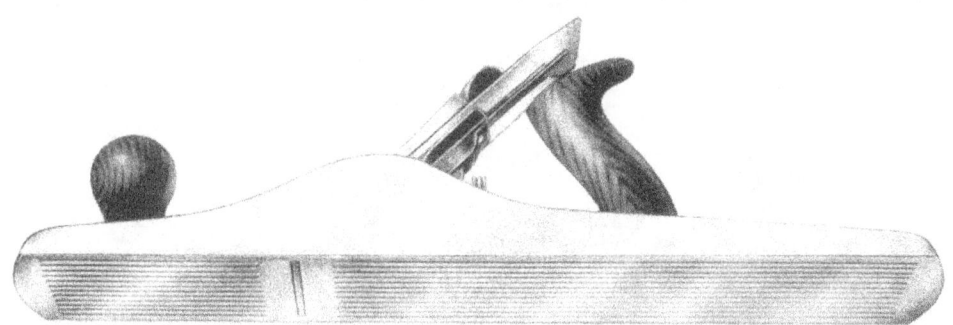

RECORD FORE AND JOINTER PLANES, with Corrugated Base.

Plane No.	Type	Price each	Length Inches	Width of Cutter Inches	Weight Pounds	Code Word
06C	Fore	22/6	18	$2\frac{3}{8}$	7	Ipmif
07C	Jointer	27/–	22	$2\frac{3}{8}$	8	Ipmog
08C	Jointer	32/–	24	$2\frac{5}{8}$	9	Ipmyk

Plane Irons and Plane Parts on pages 49 and 54.

All Planes packed 1 per box.

RECORD WORKS - - SHEFFIELD, ENGLAND

C. & J. HAMPTON, LTD. - - MANUFACTURERS

RECORD ADJUSTABLE IRON PLANES

With Warranted Best Crucible Cast
TUNGSTEN STEEL Cutting Irons.

End and Side Adjustment of Cutters.
Handles and Knobs of Selected Rosewood.
Lever Caps and Small Screws Nickel Plated.

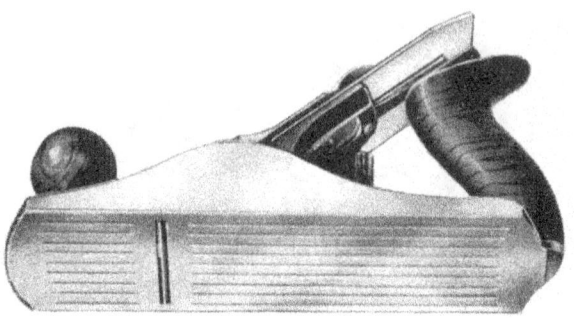

RECORD SMOOTH PLANES, with Corrugated Base.

Plane No.	Type	Price each	Length Inches	Width of Cutter Inches	Weight Pounds	Code Word
02C	Smooth	13/6	$7\frac{1}{4}$	$1\frac{5}{8}$	$2\frac{3}{8}$	Ipkia
03C	Smooth	14/–	8	$1\frac{3}{4}$	$3\frac{1}{4}$	Ipkak
04C	Smooth	14/6	9	2	$3\frac{3}{4}$	Ipkel
$04\frac{1}{2}$C	Smooth	17/–	10	$2\frac{3}{8}$	$4\frac{3}{4}$	Ipkob

RECORD JACK PLANES, with Corrugated Base.

Plane No.	Type	Price each	Length Inches	Width of Cutter Inches	Weight Pounds	Code Word
05C	Jack	17/6	14	2	$4\frac{3}{4}$	Iplad
$05\frac{1}{2}$C	Jack	20/–	15	$2\frac{1}{4}$	6	Iploe

Plane Irons and Plane Parts on pages 49 and 54.

All Planes packed 1 per box.

RECORD WORKS - - SHEFFIELD, ENGLAND

C. & J. HAMPTON, LTD. - - MANUFACTURERS

RECORD ADJUSTABLE IRON PLANES

Fitted with STAY-SET CAP IRON.

(Patent No. 362,743.)

Planes shown on pages 12 to 14 are fitted with STAY-SET Cap Irons, and are identical in every respect with the Planes shown on the preceding pages with the exception of the Cap Iron.

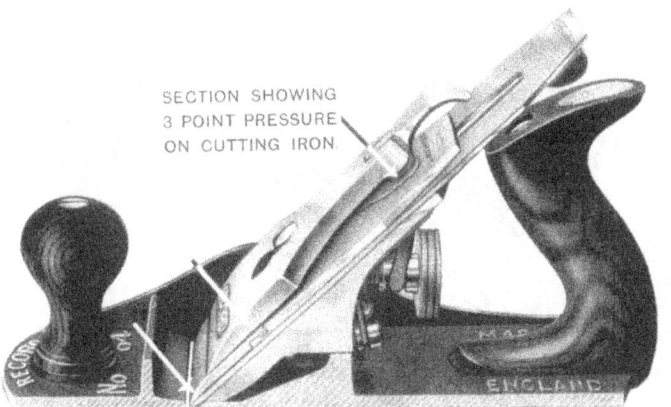

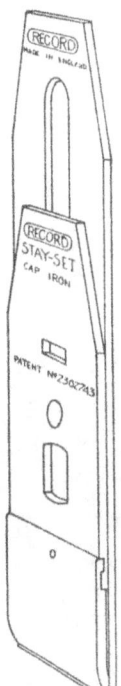

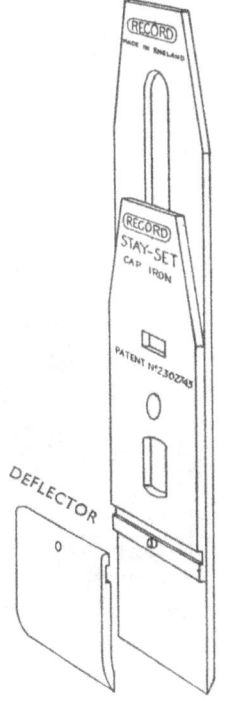

The Record STAY-SET Cap Iron is an important improvement to Adjustable Iron Planes, the advantages of which are as follows :—

1. The Cutter can be honed or sharpened without unscrewing or removing the Cap Iron. The Deflector is simply lifted clear of the Cutter to allow it to be sharpened, and when replaced the same setting is maintained without any adjustment. The Cutter can be honed many times before it is necessary to reset the Cap Iron.

2. The application of the pressure at three points on the Cutting Iron adds greatly to the rigidity of the Plane, and eliminates all possibility of chatter.

3. The STAY-SET Cap Iron is greater in thickness and is in close contact with the Cutting Iron for the whole of its length, which greatly increases the solidity and firmness of the entire cutting unit.

4. The extra thickness of the Cap Iron also provides for a longer threaded hole for the cap screw.

RECORD WORKS - - SHEFFIELD, ENGLAND

C. & J. HAMPTON, LTD. - - MANUFACTURERS

RECORD ADJUSTABLE IRON PLANES

Fitted with STAY-SET Cap Irons and
TUNGSTEN STEEL Cutters.

End and Side Adjustment of Cutters.
Handles and Knobs of Selected Rosewood.
Lever Caps and Small Screws Nickel Plated.

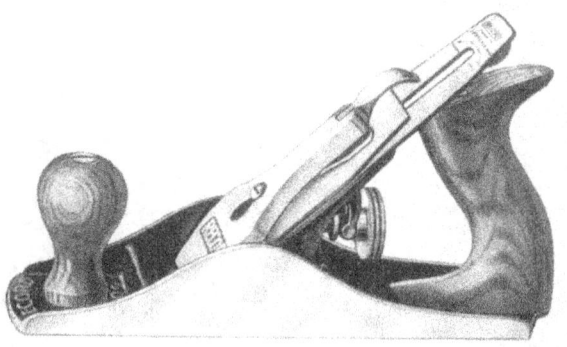

RECORD SMOOTH PLANES, with STAY-SET Cap Irons.

Plane No.	Type	Price each	Length Inches	Width of Cutter Inches	Weight Pounds	Code Word
02-SS	Smooth	12/6	$7\frac{1}{4}$	$1\frac{5}{8}$	$2\frac{3}{8}$	Istak
03-SS	Smooth	13/-	8	$1\frac{3}{4}$	$3\frac{1}{4}$	Istel
04-SS	Smooth	13/6	9	2	$3\frac{3}{4}$	Istha
$04\frac{1}{2}$-SS	Smooth	16/-	10	$2\frac{3}{8}$	$4\frac{3}{4}$	Istib

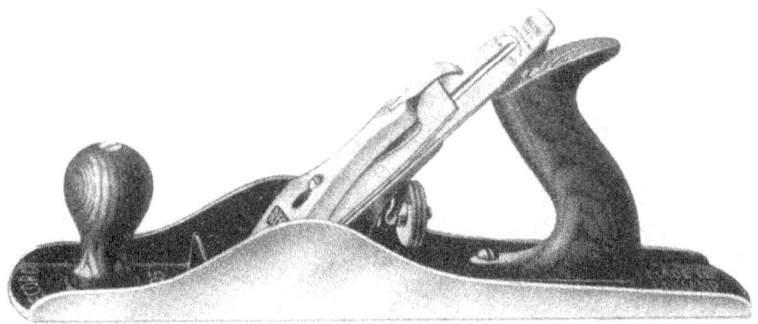

RECORD JACK PLANES, with STAY-SET Cap Irons.

Plane No.	Type	Price each	Length Inches	Width of Cutter Inches	Weight Pounds	Code Word
05-SS	Jack	16/6	14	2	$4\frac{3}{4}$	Istoc
$05\frac{1}{2}$-SS	Jack	18/6	15	$2\frac{1}{4}$	6	Istud

Plane Irons and Plane Parts on pages 49 and 54.

All Planes packed 1 per box.

RECORD WORKS - - SHEFFIELD, ENGLAND

C. & J. HAMPTON, LTD. - - MANUFACTURERS

RECORD ADJUSTABLE IRON PLANES

Fitted with STAY-SET Cap Irons and
TUNGSTEN STEEL Cutters.

End and Side Adjustment of Cutters.
Handles and Knobs of Selected Rosewood.
Lever Caps and Small Screws Nickel Plated.

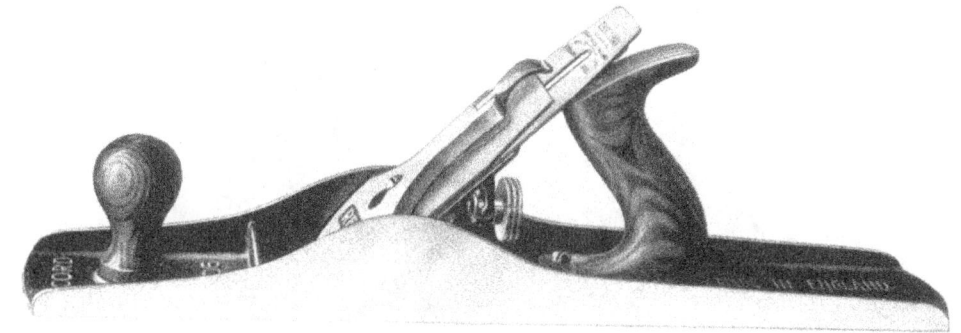

RECORD FORE AND JOINTER PLANES, with STAY-SET Cap Irons.

Plane No.	Type	Price each	Length Inches	Width of Cutter inches	Weight Pounds	Code Word
06-SS	Fore	21/–	18	$2\frac{3}{8}$	7	Istye
07-SS	Jointer	25/–	22	$2\frac{3}{8}$	8	Isnaf
08-SS	Jointer	30/–	24	$2\frac{5}{8}$	9	Isueg

RECORD FORE AND JOINTER PLANES, with Corrugated Base and STAY-SET Cap Irons.

Plane No.	Type	Price each	Length Inches	Width of Cutter Inches	Weight Pounds	Code Word
06C-SS	Fore	22/6	18	$2\frac{3}{8}$	7	Ivcez
07C-SS	Jointer	27/–	22	$2\frac{3}{8}$	8	Ivcyn
08C-SS	Jointer	32/–	24	$2\frac{5}{8}$	9	Ivdop

Plane Irons and Plane Parts on pages 49 and 54.

All Planes packed 1 per box.

RECORD WORKS - - SHEFFIELD, ENGLAND

C. & J. HAMPTON, LTD. - - MANUFACTURERS

RECORD ADJUSTABLE IRON PLANES

Fitted with STAY-SET Cap Irons and
TUNGSTEN STEEL Cutters.

End and Side Adjustment of Cutters.
Handles and Knobs of Selected Rosewood.
Lever Caps and Small Screws Nickel Plated.

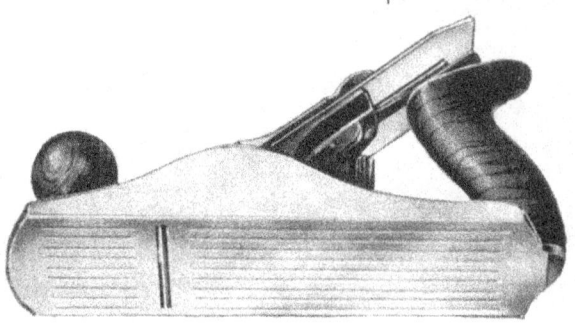

RECORD SMOOTH PLANES, with Corrugated Base and STAY-SET Cap Irons.

Plane No.	Type	Price each	Length Inches	Width of Cutter Inches	Weight Pounds	Code Word
02C-SS	Smooth	13/6	$7\frac{1}{4}$	$1\frac{5}{8}$	$2\frac{3}{8}$	Ivaro
03C-SS	Smooth	14/-	8	$1\frac{3}{4}$	$3\frac{1}{4}$	Ivasp
04C-SS	Smooth	14/6	9	2	$3\frac{3}{4}$	Ivbir
$04\frac{1}{2}$C-SS	Smooth	17/-	10	$2\frac{3}{8}$	$4\frac{3}{4}$	Ivbos

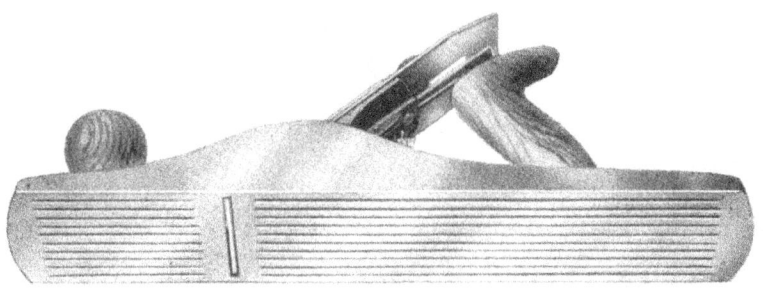

RECORD JACK PLANES, with Corrugated Base and STAY-SET Cap Irons.

Plane No.	Type	Price each	Length Inches	Width of Cutter Inches	Weight Pounds	Code Word
05C-SS	Jack	17/6	14	2	$4\frac{3}{4}$	Ivbut
$05\frac{1}{2}$C-SS	Jack	20/-	15	$2\frac{1}{4}$	6	Ivcav

Plane Irons and Plane Parts on pages 49 and 54.

All Planes packed 1 per box.

RECORD WORKS - - SHEFFIELD, ENGLAND

C. & J. HAMPTON, LTD. - - MANUFACTURERS

RECORD RABBET PLANES
For Carriage Makers

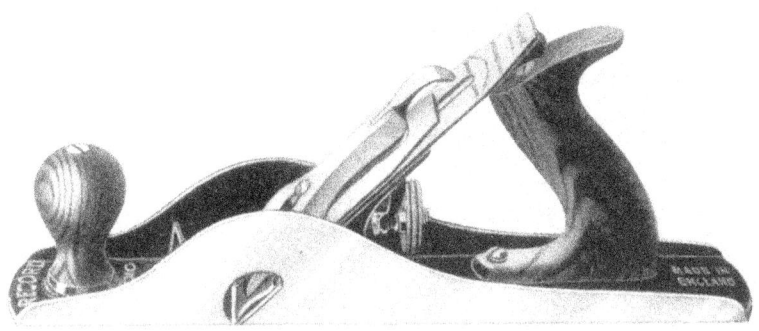

These Planes have Malleable Iron Bodies, and are practically unbreakable.
They are recommended for carriage and wagon building and similar heavy work.
End and Side Adjustment of Cutters. Handles and Knobs of Selected Rosewood.
Lever Caps and Small Screws Nickel Plated.

Plane No.	Price each	Length Inches	Width of Cutter Inches	Weight Pounds	Code Word
010½	21/6	9	2⅛	3¼	Ipesu
010	23/-	13	2⅛	4¼	Ipeep

RECORD DUPLEX RABBET and FILLETSTER PLANES, No. 078

No. 078 Plane has two positions for the Cutter, one for ordinary work, and the other for bull-nose work.

It is fitted with a hardened steel spur, an adjustable depth gauge which is removable, and an adjustable Fence which can be used on either side of the Plane.

This Plane is adaptable for many other purposes besides Rabbeting when the Fence and Arm are removed.

The Cutter, when used in the rear position, is adjusted endwise by a lever.

The base and sides are ground and polished, and the fittings nickel-plated.

8½" long.   1½" Cutter.   Weight 3 pounds.   Code Word: Ipert.
PRICE   ...   **11/3** each.

Plane Irons and Plane Parts on pages 50, 54 and 55.

All Planes packed 1 per box.

RECORD WORKS - - SHEFFIELD, ENGLAND

C. & J. HAMPTON, LTD. - - MANUFACTURERS

RECORD BULL-NOSE RABBET PLANES

No. 075

For planing into corners and difficult positions. The Mouth is adjustable.
4" long.   1" Cutter.   Weight ⅝ pound.   Code Word : Ipeps.

PRICE   ...   **2/6** each.

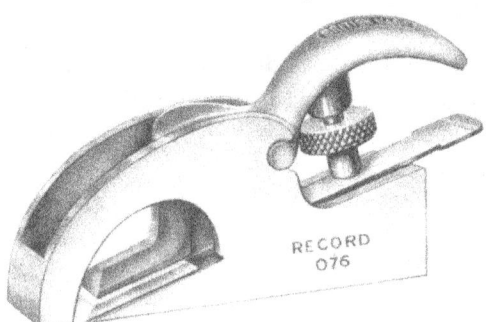

No. 076. Non-Adjustable.

The base and sides of these Planes are accurately machined and ground.
They are fitted with Tungsten Steel Cutters.
4" long.   1⅛" Cutter.   Weight 1 pound.   Code Word : Ipnud.

PRICE   ...   **6/3** each.

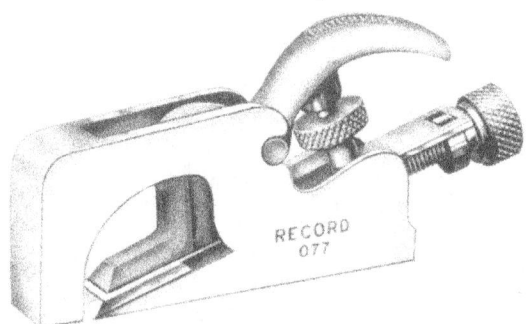

No. 077. Adjustable. Nickel Plated.

These Planes are for fine work where extreme accuracy is required.
The base and sides are accurately machined and ground.
They have Screw Adjustment for regulating the depth of cut, and are fitted with
Tungsten Steel Cutters. Packed in varnished wood box with sliding lid.
4" long.   1⅛" Cutter.   Weight 1¼ pounds.   Code Word : Ipnye.

PRICE   ...   **10/-** each.

Plane Irons and Plane Parts on pages 50 and 56.   All Planes packed 1 per box.

RECORD WORKS - - SHEFFIELD, ENGLAND

C. & J. HAMPTON, LTD. - - MANUFACTURERS

RECORD IMPROVED
BULL-NOSE RABBET PLANES

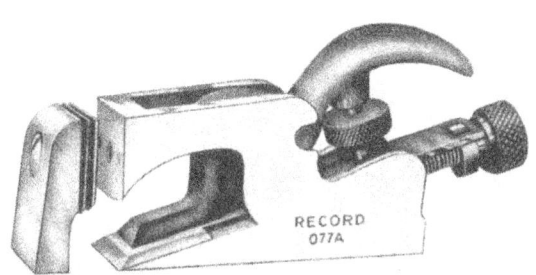

No. 077A. Nickel Plated.

With Cutter and Mouth Adjustment and Detachable Nose.

This Plane is for fine work where extreme accuracy is required.

The base and sides are accurately machined and ground.

An improved Adjustable Mouth has been embodied in this Plane by fitting two steel distance pieces in between the Detachable Nose and the Plane Body, which gives four varying openings for fine or coarse work.

It can be used as a Chisel Plane by removing the Nose.

It has Screw Adjustment for regulating the depth of cut, and is fitted with Tungsten Steel Cutter.

4" long. $1\frac{1}{8}$" Cutter.   Weight $1\frac{1}{4}$ pounds.   Code Word : Ipolf.

PRICE   ...   **11/6** each.

Plane Irons and Plane Parts on pages 50 and 56.

Packed in varnished wood box with sliding lid.

RECORD WORKS - - SHEFFIELD, ENGLAND

C. & J. HAMPTON, LTD.   -   -   MANUFACTURERS

RECORD "THREE-IN-ONE"
BULL NOSE and SHOULDER RABBET PLANES
No. 311

With Cutter Adjustment.

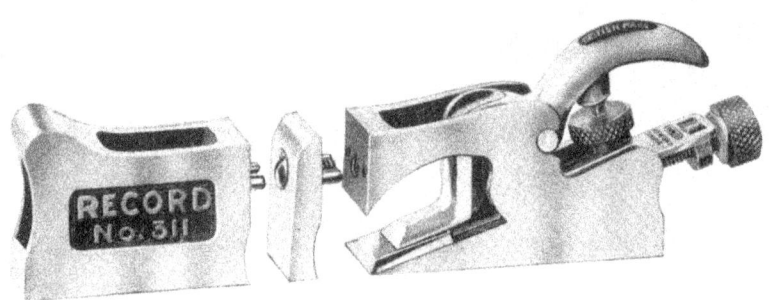

Nickel Plated.

Record "Three-in-One" Plane—Shoulder Rabbet, Bull Nose Rabbet and Chisel Plane.

These Planes have screw adjustment on the cutter for regulating the depth of cut and are fitted with Tungsten Steel Cutters.

6" long. $1\frac{1}{8}$" Cutter.   Weight 2 pounds.   Code Word : Iraft.

PRICE COMPLETE ... **16/6** each.

Plane Irons and Plane Parts on pages 50 and 56.

Packed in varnished wood box with sliding lid.

RECORD WORKS   -   -   SHEFFIELD, ENGLAND

C. & J. HAMPTON, LTD.   -   -   MANUFACTURERS

RECORD SKEW RABBET PLANES

With Adjustable Depth Gauge and
Tungsten Steel Cutter.

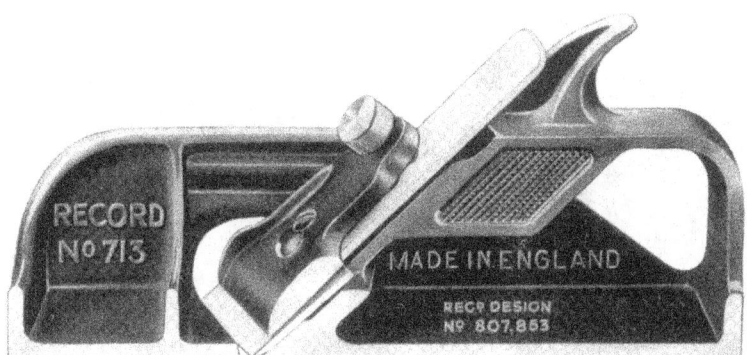

Registered Design No. 807,853.

The skew cutter in this Plane, together with the perfect balance, ensures smooth cutting with very little effort.

It will lie perfectly flat on either side, and is fitted with an Adjustable Depth Gauge which can be detached when necessary.

The skew cutter also enables the Plane to be used for rabbeting across the grain.

Plane No.	Price each	Length Inches	Width of Cutter Inches	Weight Pounds	Code Word
712	7/-	$8\frac{5}{8}$	$1\frac{1}{4}$	$2\frac{1}{2}$	Irbas
713	7/9	$8\frac{5}{8}$	$1\frac{1}{2}$	$2\frac{3}{4}$	Irbet
714	8/6	$8\frac{5}{8}$	$1\frac{3}{4}$	3	Irbiu

Plane Irons and Plane Parts on pages 51 and 57.

All Planes packed 1 per box.

RECORD WORKS   -   -   SHEFFIELD, ENGLAND

C. & J. HAMPTON, LTD.   -   -   MANUFACTURERS

RECORD IMPROVED SHOULDER RABBET PLANES

With Cutter and Mouth Adjustment

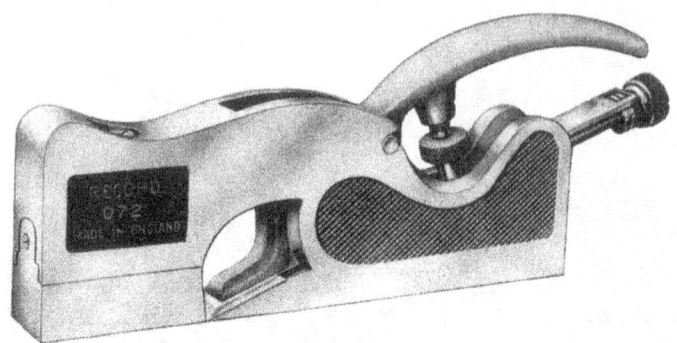

Nickel Plated.

These Planes are for very fine and accurate work. The base and sides are accurately machined and ground. They will lie quite flat on either side, and can be used both right and left hand.

An improved Screw Adjustment to the Mouth has been embodied in these Planes, Nos. 072, 073 and 074, which gives a wide range of adjustment for either fine or coarse work.

They have Screw Adjustment on the Cutter for regulating the depth of cut, and are fitted with Tungsten Steel Cutters.

Plane No.	Price each	Length Inches	Width of Cutter Inches	Weight Pounds	Code Word
*041	11/6	5	$\frac{5}{8}$	$1\frac{1}{4}$	Iraso
*042	16/6	8	$\frac{3}{4}$	$2\frac{3}{4}$	Irayr
072	19/6	$8\frac{1}{8}$	1	$3\frac{1}{4}$	Ipnal
073	22/6	$8\frac{1}{8}$	$1\frac{1}{4}$	4	Ipnib
074	25/6	$8\frac{1}{8}$	$1\frac{1}{2}$	$4\frac{3}{4}$	Ipnoc

* Nos. 041 and 042 are made only with Non-Adjustable Mouth.
Plane Irons and Plane Parts on pages 50 and 56.

Packed in varnished wood box with sliding lid.

RECORD WORKS   -   -   SHEFFIELD, ENGLAND

C. & J. HAMPTON, LTD. - - MANUFACTURERS

RECORD SIDE RABBET PLANES
No. 2506

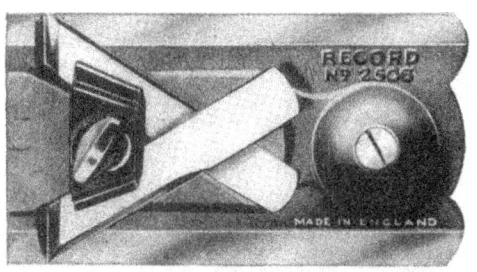

Nickel Plated.

For side rabbeting and cleaning grooves in mouldings, etc.
The Nose can be removed for working close up into corners.

Weight $\frac{5}{8}$ pound.   Code Word : Ircep.

PRICE   ...   8/- each.

No. 2506S with Depth Stop.

Same as above, but with adjustable and reversible Depth Stop fitted to the base.

Weight $\frac{5}{8}$ pound.   Code Word : Ircir.

PRICE   ...   10/- each.

RECORD BULL-NOSE RABBET PLANES
No. 1366

Nickel Plated, with Rosewood Wedge.

3" long. $\frac{3}{8}$" Cutter.   Weight 5 ounces.   Code Word : Ircos.

PRICE   ...   5/6 each.

Plane Irons on page 50.

All Planes packed 1 per box.

RECORD WORKS - - SHEFFIELD, ENGLAND

C. & J. HAMPTON, LTD. - - MANUFACTURERS

RECORD CIRCULAR PLANES

These Circular Planes are fitted with flexible spring steel faces for planing concave and convex surfaces. End and Side Adjustment of Cutters.

No. 020

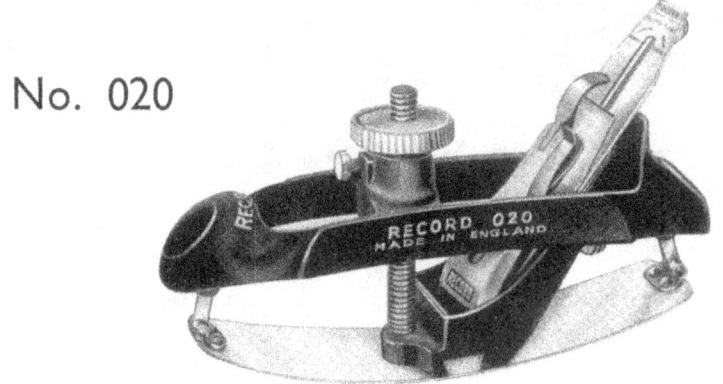

The steel face of **No. 020** Plane is anchored at each end to the body, and is screw adjusted from the centre. Frame provides handles at both ends.

10″ long.   1¾″ Cutter.   Weight 4 pounds.   Code Word : Ipfer.

PRICE   ...   **27/-** each.

No. 0113

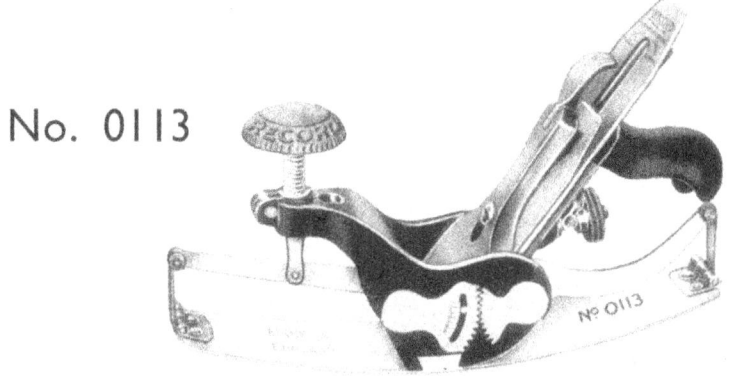

The steel face of **No. 0113** Plane is anchored to the Plane Body in the centre and adjusted at the ends by means of a screw controlling the two levers. The toothed segment plates are graduated to provide for setting to correct radii.

10″ long.   1¾″ Cutter.   Weight 3¾ pounds.   Code Word : Ipfis.

PRICE   ...   **27/-** each.

Plane Irons and Plane Parts on pages 50 and 58.

All Planes packed 1 per box.

RECORD WORKS - - SHEFFIELD, ENGLAND

C. & J. HAMPTON, LTD. - - MANUFACTURERS

RECORD SCRUB PLANES
No. 400½

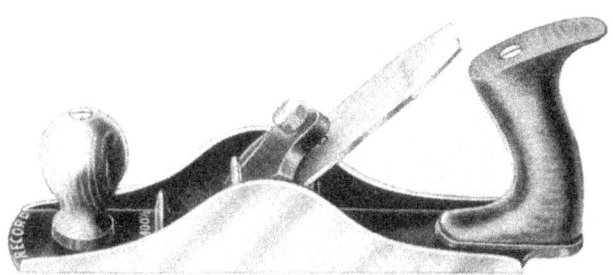

This Plane is used for coarse work such as "hogging" down timber to rough dimensions.

The cutter is of extra thickness and the cutting edge is rounded for heavy work. Handle and knob are of beechwood.

10½″ long.   1½″ Cutter.   Weight 2½ pounds.   Code Word : Ipgua.

PRICE   ...   **10/6** each.

Plane Irons on page 51.

RECORD ROUTER PLANES
No. 722

These Planes are for cutting grooves, etc., parallel to the surface of the work. Two holes are provided in the body into which the cutter can be inserted.

¼″ width of Cutter.   Weight ¾ pound.   Code Word : Irebs.

PRICE   ...   **3/6** each.

Plane Irons on page 50.

All Planes packed 1 per box.

RECORD WORKS - - SHEFFIELD, ENGLAND

C. & J. HAMPTON, LTD. - - MANUFACTURERS

RECORD ROUTER PLANES
No. 071

OPEN THROAT. With Improved Adjustable Fence.

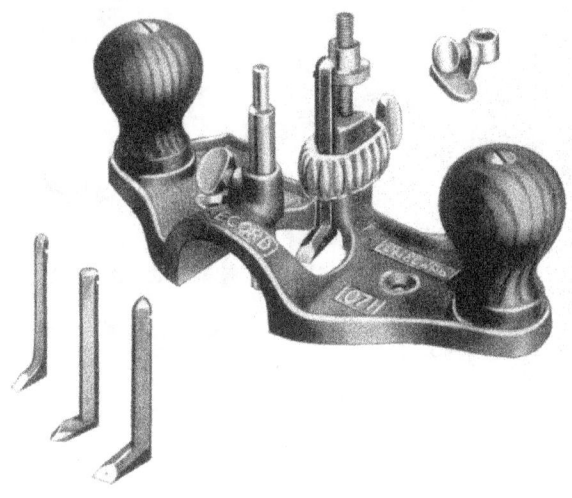

These Planes are for cutting grooves, etc., parallel to the surface of the work. The improved Fence enables grooves to be cut parallel to the edge of the work whether straight or circular.

The Fence is adjustable and can be used either right or left hand.

The Cutters are adjustable by Screw Feed, and can be secured on the front of the Cutter Post for general work or on the back for Bull Nose work.

For narrow surfaces there is an Adjustable Shoe and Gauge for closing the throat and also for regulating the depth of cut.

An extra wooden bottom can be attached to the Plane for routering wide grooves.

Showing Fence in position.

$7\frac{1}{2}''$ long.   Beech Knobs.

3 Cutters, $\frac{1}{4}''$, $\frac{1}{2}''$, and Smoothing Cutter.

Weight $2\frac{1}{4}$ pounds.   Code Word : Ipfot.

PRICE complete **15/-** each.

Plane Irons and Plane Parts on pages 50 and 58.

All Planes packed 1 per box.

RECORD WORKS - - SHEFFIELD, ENGLAND

C. & J. HAMPTON, LTD. - - MANUFACTURERS

RECORD ROUTER PLANES
No. 071½

CLOSED THROAT.   With Improved Adjustable Fence.

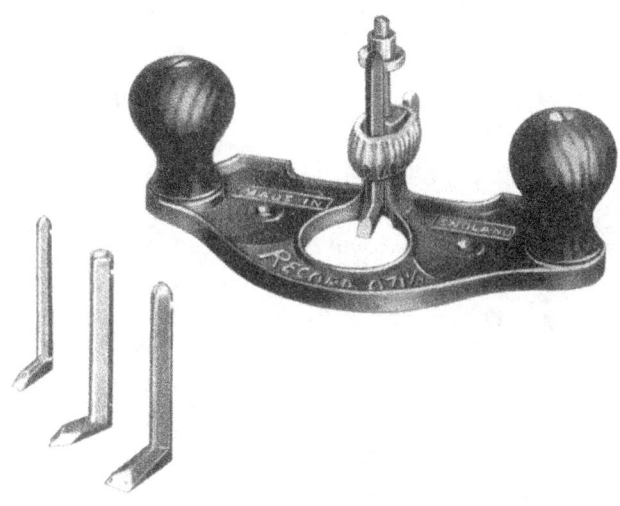

These Planes are for cutting grooves, etc., parallel to the surface of the work. The improved Fence enables grooves to be cut parallel to the edge of the work whether straight or circular.

The Fence is adjustable and can be used either right or left hand.

The Cutters are adjustable by Screw Feed, and can be secured on the front of the Cutter Post for general work or on the back for Bull Nose work.

An extra wooden bottom can be attached to the Plane for routering wide grooves.

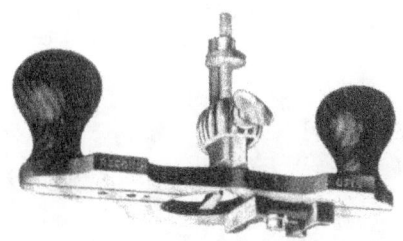

7½" long.   Beech Knobs.
3 Cutters, ¼", ½", and Smoothing Cutter.
Weight 2 pounds.   Code Word: Ipfru.
PRICE complete **12/-** each.

Showing Fence in position.

Plane Irons and Plane Parts on pages 50 and 58.

All Planes packed 1 per box.

RECORD WORKS - - SHEFFIELD, ENGLAND

C. & J. HAMPTON, LTD. - - MANUFACTURERS

RECORD PLOUGH PLANES

Record Plough Plane, No. 040, with 3 Tungsten Steel Cutters.

This Plane is suitable for grooving for Plywood Panels, etc. It is fitted with Adjustable Depth Gauge and Single Arm Fence, and will cut grooves $\frac{1}{2}''$ deep up to 3" from edge.

Three Plough Cutters are supplied with each Plane, viz., $\frac{1}{8}''$, $\frac{3}{16}''$, and $\frac{1}{4}''$.

Body cellulosed Blue.   Nickel Plated Fittings.

$5\frac{1}{2}''$ long.   Weight 1 pound.   Code Word : Ipvon.

PRICE COMPLETE ... **6/6** each.

Record Plough Plane, No. 043, with 3 Tungsten Steel Cutters.

Nickel Plated.

This Plane is suitable for grooving for Plywood Panels, etc. It is fitted with Adjustable Depth Gauge and Double Arm Bridged Fence, and will cut grooves $\frac{1}{2}''$ deep up to 4" from edge.

Three Plough Cutters are supplied with each Plane, viz., $\frac{1}{8}''$, $\frac{3}{16}''$, and $\frac{1}{4}''$.

$5\frac{1}{2}''$ long.   Weight $1\frac{1}{4}$ pounds.   Code Word : Ipwup.

PRICE COMPLETE ... **9/6** each.

ADDITIONAL CUTTERS for above Planes.

For grooving for Plywood Panels, etc., Cutters of millimetre width are available as below :—

Size	4	6	9	12 m/m wide.
Each	1/3	1/3	1/9	1/9

Plane Parts on page 59.   All Planes packed 1 per box.

RECORD WORKS - - SHEFFIELD, ENGLAND

C. & J. HAMPTON, LTD.   -   -   MANUFACTURERS

RECORD PLOUGH PLANES
Nos. 040 and 043

The cross sections illustrated are examples of work which can be performed by the Nos. 040 and 043 Planes.

Plane No. 043 has a greater capacity from the edge of the wood and can be used either right or left hand.

Both Planes will plough end grain as well as long grain. The narrow face of the fence allows narrow boards to be ploughed in the Vice. When a deep fence is required, a parallel fillet of hard wood can be screwed on to the fence.

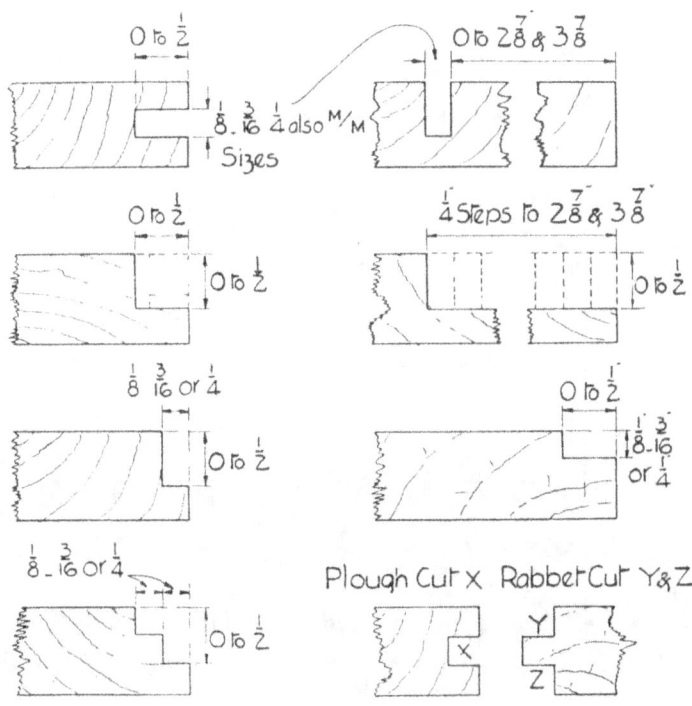

RECORD WORKS   -   -   SHEFFIELD, ENGLAND

C. & J. HAMPTON, LTD.   -   -   MANUFACTURERS

RECORD PLOUGH PLANE
No. 044

With Screw Adjustment to Cutter.

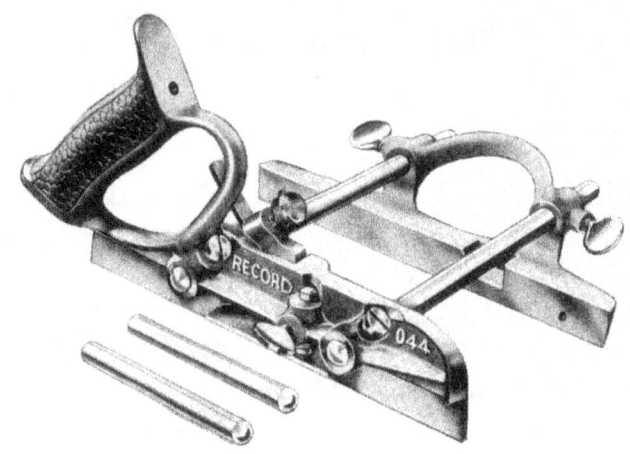

Registered Design No. 811,133.
Nickel Plated.

No. 044 Plough Plane with 8 Tungsten Steel Cutters.

This Plane is fitted with Adjustable Depth Gauge, Double Arm adjustable Bridged Fence and 2 pairs of Fence Arms (long and short), and will cut grooves $\frac{5}{8}''$ deep up to 5" from edge.

Screw adjustment is fitted to the Cutter which enables it to be fed into the work with an accurate and easy control.

Eight Plough Cutters are supplied with each Plane, as illustrated.

$8\frac{1}{2}''$ long.   Weight $2\frac{3}{4}$ pounds.   Code Word : Ipvim.

PRICE COMPLETE ... **17/6** each.

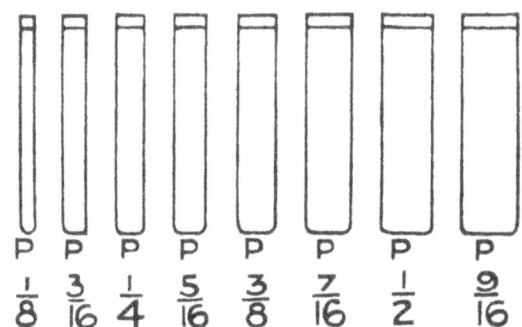

Price for EXTRA Cutters—
1/- 1/- 1/3 1/3 1/9 1/9 1/9 1/9 each.

ADDITIONAL CUTTERS of millimetre width for grooving for Plywood Panels, etc., are available, as below :—

Size	...	...	...	...	4	6	9	12 m/m wide.
Each	...	...	...	...	1/3	1/3	1/9	1/9

Plane Parts on page 59.   All Planes packed 1 per box.

RECORD WORKS   -   -   SHEFFIELD, ENGLAND

C. & J. HAMPTON, LTD. - - MANUFACTURERS

RECORD PLOUGH PLANE
No. 044

The cross sections illustrate examples of work which can be performed with the No. 044 Plane.

The fence can be used on either side, and the face of the fence can be increased in depth by screwing on a hard wood fillet.

All cuts made by the Nos. 040 and 043 Planes can also be made with the No. 044, and many more in addition, due to greater capacity and more cutters.

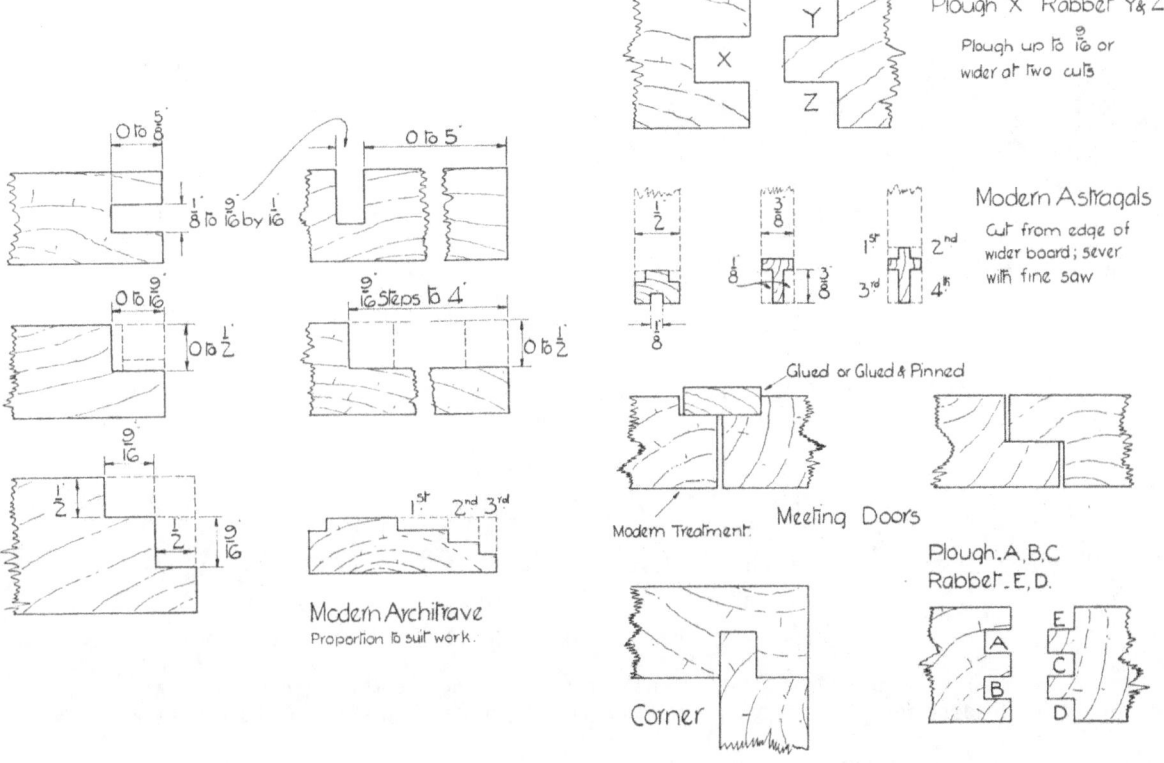

RECORD WORKS - - SHEFFIELD, ENGLAND

C. & J. HAMPTON, LTD. - - MANUFACTURERS

RECORD IMPROVED COMBINATION PLANE
No. 050A

With Cutter Screw Adjustment and Narrow Cutter Clamping Bracket.

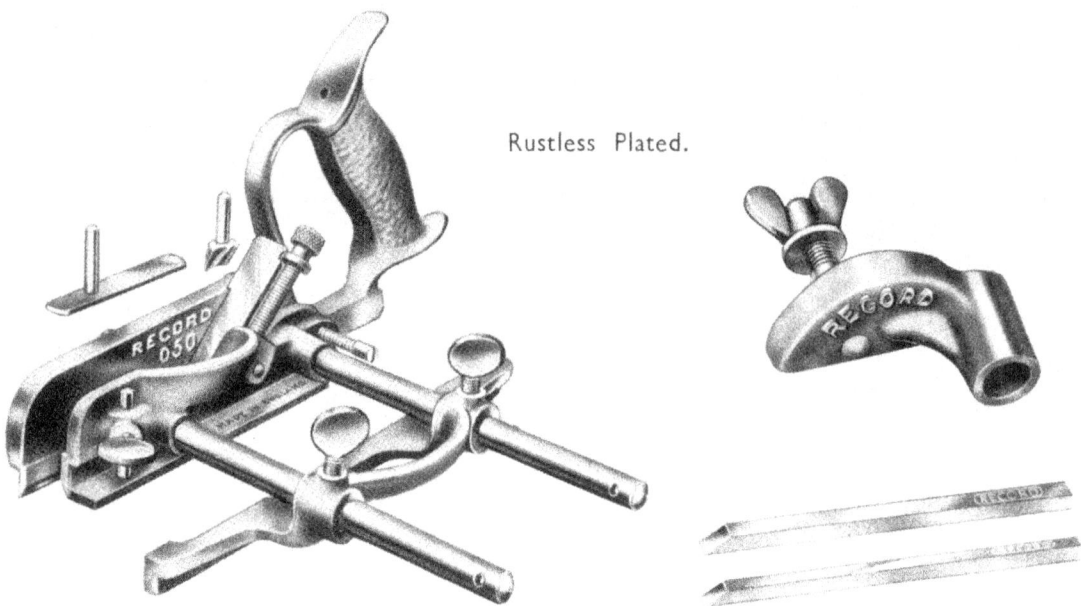

Rustless Plated.

No. 050A with 17 Tungsten Steel Cutters.

The **No. 050A** Record Combination Plane is a combined tool which will perform most planing operations generally required in cabinet making and joinery, namely,

1. Ploughing.
2. Dadoing.
3. Beading.
4. Centre Beading.
5. Rabbeting and Filletstering.
6. Tonguing and Grooving.

It is fitted with spurs for cross-grain work, adjustable depth gauge, double arm adjustable bridged fence, beading stop and also shaving deflector for use when tonguing.

It will plough or rabbet $\frac{1}{2}''$ deep up to 5'' from edge.

The face of the fence can be increased in depth by screwing on a hardwood fillet.

Continued

RECORD WORKS - - SHEFFIELD, ENGLAND

C. & J. HAMPTON, LTD. - - MANUFACTURERS

RECORD IMPROVED COMBINATION PLANE
No. 050A

The Record Improved Combination Plane is fitted with Screw Adjustment to the Cutter, which enables it to be fed into the work with an accurate and easy control.

A complete set of 15 Cutters, as illustrated, is supplied with this Plane, and in addition a Clamping Bracket and a Plough Cutter, each $\frac{1}{8}''$ and $\frac{3}{16}''$ wide. With this improved feature grooves narrower than $\frac{1}{4}''$ can be ploughed suitable for plywood panels, etc.

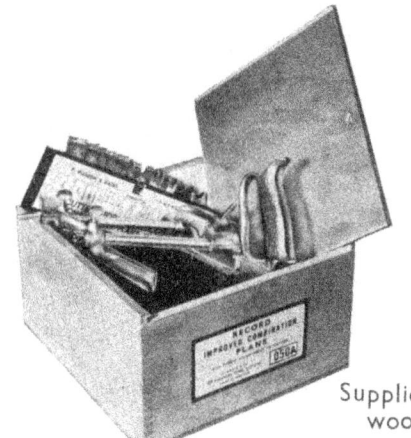

$9\frac{1}{4}''$ long.   Weight $3\frac{3}{4}$ pounds.

Code Word : Ipfuy.

PRICE COMPLETE ... **30/-** each.

Instruction Book provided with each Plane.

Supplied complete in varnished wood box with sliding lid.

The following Cutters are supplied with Record Improved Combination Planes, but should extra Cutters be required, they are available at extra charge.

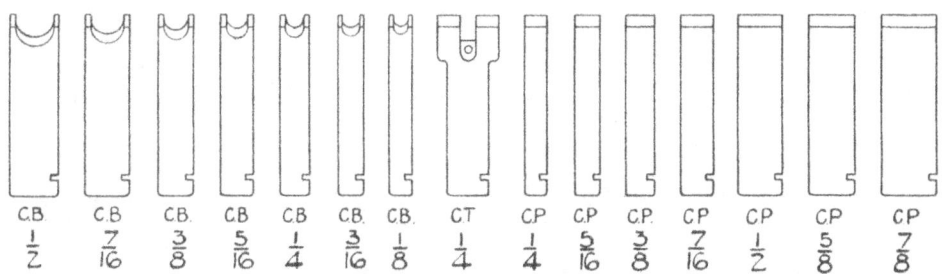

| C.B. $\frac{1}{2}$ | C.B. $\frac{7}{16}$ | C.B. $\frac{3}{8}$ | C.B. $\frac{5}{16}$ | C.B. $\frac{1}{4}$ | C.B. $\frac{3}{16}$ | C.B. $\frac{1}{8}$ | C.T. $\frac{1}{4}$ | C.P. $\frac{1}{4}$ | C.P. $\frac{5}{16}$ | C.P. $\frac{3}{8}$ | C.P. $\frac{7}{16}$ | C.P. $\frac{1}{2}$ | C.P. $\frac{5}{8}$ | C.P. $\frac{7}{8}$ |

Price for EXTRA Cutters—

2/-   2/-   1/9   1/9   1/3   1/3   1/3   4/3   1/3   1/3   1/9   1/9   1/9   1/9   2/- each.

Plough Cutters, $\frac{1}{8}''$ C.P. and $\frac{3}{16}''$ C.P. for use with Clamping Bracket ... 1/3 each.

ADDITIONAL CUTTERS of millimetre width for grooving for Plywood Panels, etc., are available, as below :—

| Size | ... | ... | 4 | 6 | 9 | 12 m/m wide. |
| Price each | ... | ... | 1/3 | 1/3 | 1/9 | 1/9 |

Tonguing Cutters, $\frac{1}{8}''$ and $\frac{3}{16}''$, are available ... 4/3 each.

Plane Parts on page 60.

RECORD WORKS - - SHEFFIELD, ENGLAND

C. & J. HAMPTON, LTD. - - MANUFACTURERS

RECORD IMPROVED COMBINATION PLANE
No. 050

With Screw Adjustment to Cutter.

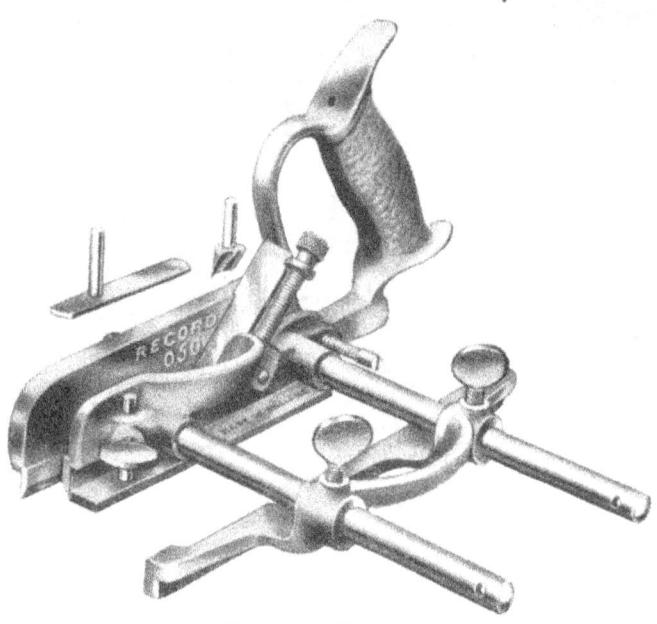

The **No. 050** Combination Plane is the same as the **No. 050A** but without the Cutter Clamping Bracket and $\frac{1}{8}''$ and $\frac{3}{16}''$ Plough Cutters.

$9\frac{1}{4}''$ long. Weight $3\frac{1}{2}$ pounds.

Code Word : Ipfap.

PRICE COMPLETE **27/6** each.

Instruction Book provided with each Plane.

Supplied complete in varnished wood box with sliding lid.

Rustless Plated.
No. 050 with 15 Tungsten Steel Cutters.

NARROW CUTTER CLAMPING BRACKET

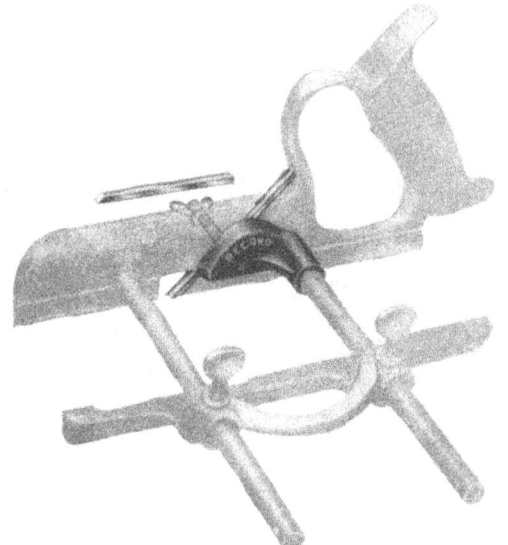

For use with the **No. 050** Record Combination Plane.

This Cutter Clamping Bracket, together with a $\frac{1}{8}''$ and $\frac{3}{16}''$ Cutter, is the same as is fitted to the **No. 050A** Plane.

This attachment with the two Cutters can be supplied to convert the **No. 050** Plane into a **No. 050A**.

PRICE complete with two Cutters, **3/-** each.

Code Word : Ipfyz.

Plane Parts on page 60.

RECORD WORKS - - SHEFFIELD, ENGLAND

C. & J. HAMPTON, LTD. - - MANUFACTURERS

RECORD IMPROVED COMBINATION PLANES
Nos. 050 and 050A

The cross sections illustrated are suggestive of cuts which can be made with the Nos. 050 and 050A Planes, and also indicate the methods. In addition, all cuts shown for No. 044 and smaller Plough Planes can be made with these Combination Planes.

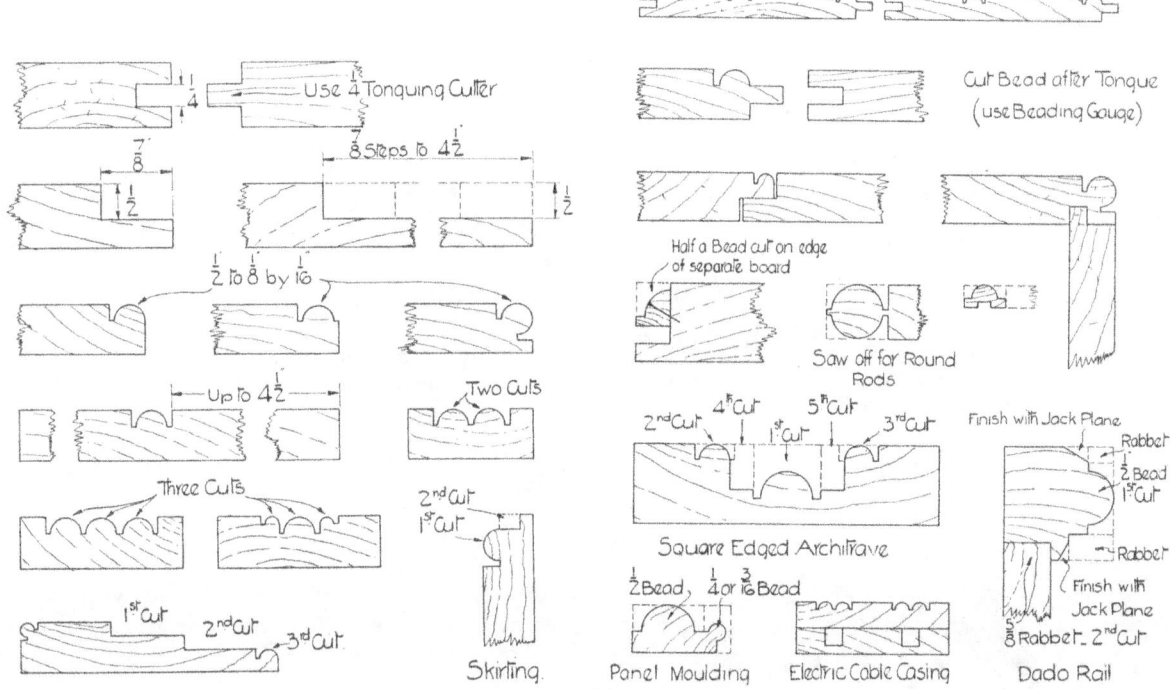

DADO CUTS, i.e., grooves across the grain, can also be performed with these Planes.

RECORD WORKS - - SHEFFIELD, ENGLAND

C. & J. HAMPTON, LTD. - - MANUFACTURERS

RECORD MULTI-PLANE, No. 405

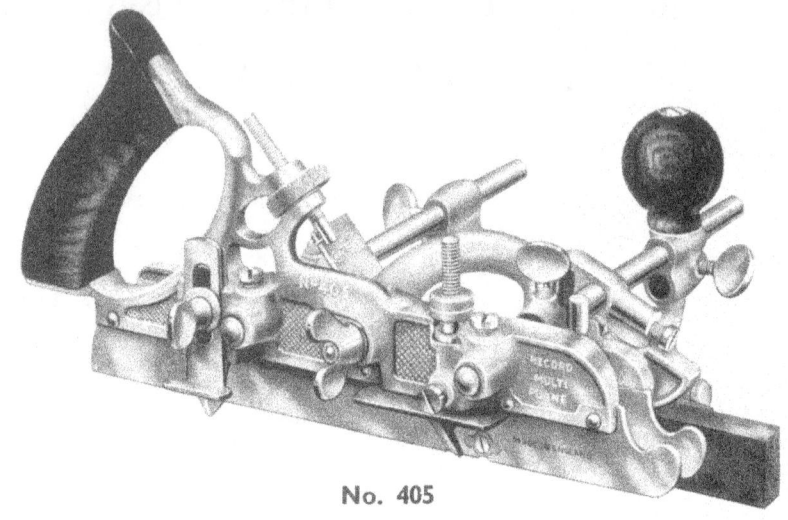

No. 405

with 23 Tungsten Steel Cutters.

The Record Multi-Plane, as the name implies, will perform many planing operations required by the Cabinet Maker and Joiner, namely,

1. Ploughing.
2. Dadoing.
3. Beading.
4. Centre Beading.
5. Rabbeting and Filletstering.
6. Match Planing.
7. Sash Planing.
8. Slitting.

The Record Multi-Plane possesses the following features :—

Screw Adjustment to the Cutter.
Screw Adjustment to the Fence.
Screw Adjustment to the Depth Gauge.
2 sets of Arms (Long and Short).
Beading Stop.

Slitting Cutter Stop.
Sliding Section Depth Gauge.
Cam Steady.
Spurs for Cross Grain Work.

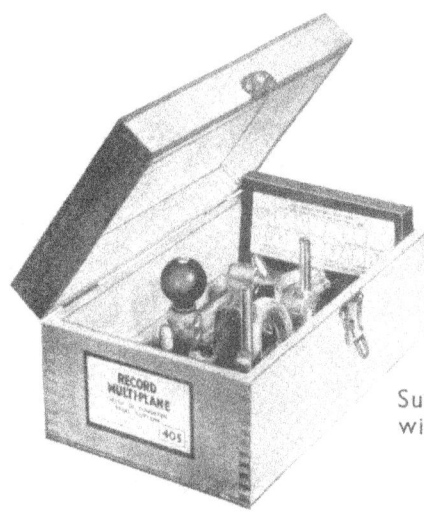

The metal parts are all Rustless Plated, and the Handle, Knob and Fence are of selected Rosewood.

23 Cutters, as illustrated, are supplied with the Plane, and additional Cutters, also shown, are available from stock at a small extra charge.

Weight $9\frac{1}{2}$ pounds.   Code Word : Iphab.

PRICE complete **60/-** each.

Instruction Book provided with each Plane.

Supplied complete in varnished wood box with chromium-plated hinges and fastener.

Plane Parts on page 61.

RECORD WORKS - - SHEFFIELD, ENGLAND

C. & J. HAMPTON, LTD. - - MANUFACTURERS

RECORD MULTI-PLANE, No. 405
STANDARD CUTTERS.

The following 23 CUTTERS ARE ALWAYS SUPPLIED with the Record Multi-Plane, but should extra Cutters be required, they are available at extra charge as listed below.

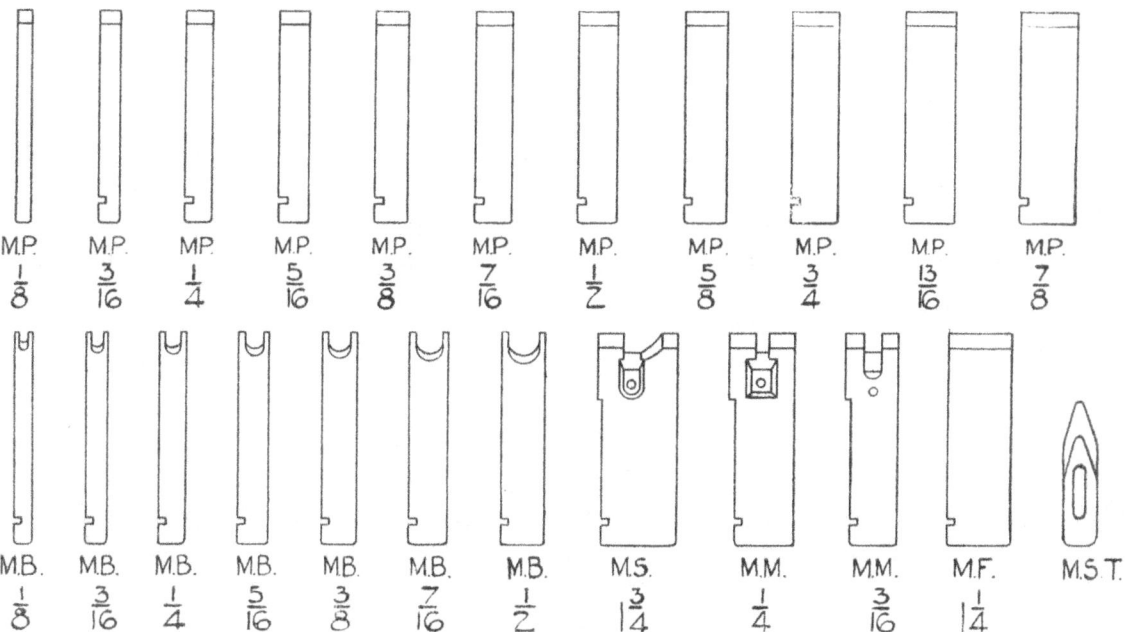

Size Inches	Type	Price Each	Size Inches	Type	Price Each
$\frac{1}{8}$	Plough and Dado Tool	1/3	$\frac{1}{8}$	Beading Tool	1/3
$\frac{3}{16}$	,, ,, ,,	1/3	$\frac{3}{16}$	,, ,,	1/3
$\frac{1}{4}$	,, ,, ,,	1/3	$\frac{1}{4}$	,, ,,	1/3
$\frac{5}{16}$	,, ,, ,,	1/3	$\frac{5}{16}$	,, ,,	1/9
$\frac{3}{8}$	,, ,, ,,	1/9	$\frac{3}{8}$	,, ,,	1/9
$\frac{7}{16}$	,, ,, ,,	1/9	$\frac{7}{16}$	,, ,,	2/-
$\frac{1}{2}$	,, ,, ,,	1/9	$\frac{1}{2}$	,, ,,	2/-
$\frac{5}{8}$	,, ,, ,,	1/9	$1\frac{3}{4}$	Sash Tool	4/3
$\frac{3}{4}$	,, ,, ,,	1/9	$\frac{1}{4}$	Match Tool	4/3
$\frac{13}{16}$	,, ,, ,,	2/-	$\frac{3}{16}$	,, ,,	4/3
$\frac{7}{8}$	,, ,, ,,	2/-	$1\frac{1}{4}$	Filletster	2/-
			—	Slitting Tool	2/6

Complete set of 23 CUTTERS as above, **29/-** per set.

RECORD WORKS - - SHEFFIELD, ENGLAND

C. & J. HAMPTON, LTD.   -   -   MANUFACTURERS

RECORD MULTI-PLANE, No. 405

ADDITIONAL CUTTERS.

ADDITIONAL CUTTERS for the Record Multi-Plane are available as below:—

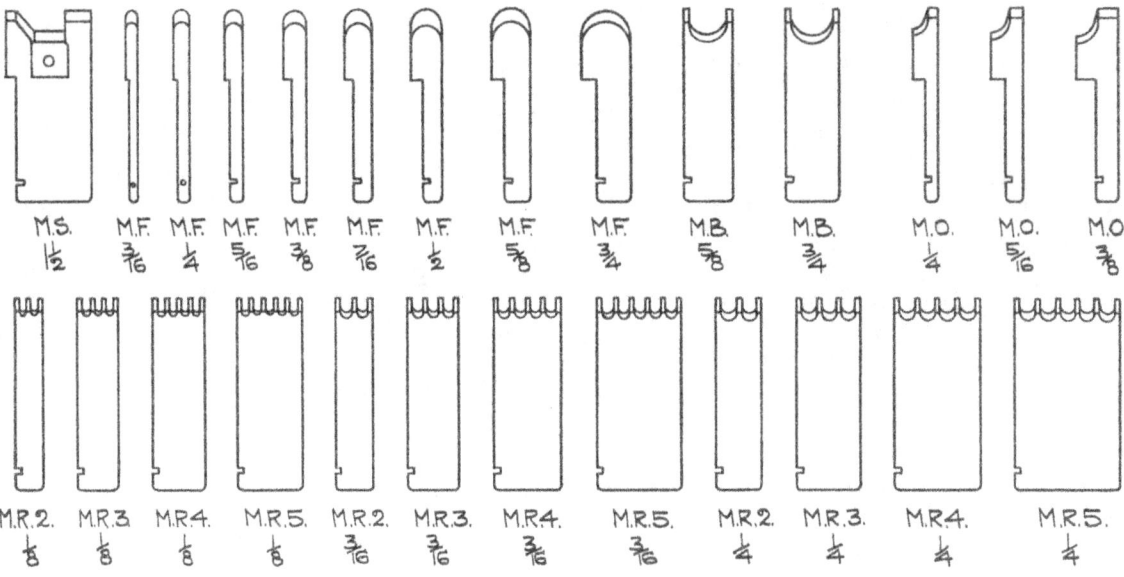

M.S.	M.F.	M.F.	M.F.	M.F.	M.F.	M.F.	M.F.	M.B.	M.B.	M.O.	M.O.	M.O.
1½	3/16	¼	5/16	3/8	7/16	½	5/8	3/4	5/8	3/4	¼	5/16	3/8

M.R.2	M.R.3	M.R.4	M.R.5	M.R.2	M.R.3	M.R.4	M.R.5	M.R.2	M.R.3	M.R.4	M.R.5
⅛	⅛	⅛	⅛	3/16	3/16	3/16	3/16	¼	¼	¼	¼

Size Inches	Type			Price Each	Size Inches	Type			Price Each
1½	Sash Tool	...	...	4/3	5/8	Beading Tool	...	...	2/6
3/16	Fluting Tool	...	...	2/6	3/4	,, ,,	...	...	2/6
¼	,, ,,	...	...	2/6	⅛	Reeding Tool, 2 Beads	...		1/9
5/16	,, ,,	...	...	2/6	⅛	,, ,, 3 ,,		...	2/6
3/8	,, ,,	...	...	2/6	⅛	,, ,, 4 ,,		...	3/3
7/16	,, ,,	...	...	2/6	⅛	,, ,, 5 ,,		...	4/3
½	,, ,,	...	...	2/6	3/16	,, ,, 2 ,,		...	1/9
5/8	,, ,,	...	...	2/6	3/16	,, ,, 3 ,,		...	2/6
3/4	,, ,,	...	...	2/6	3/16	,, ,, 4 ,,		...	3/3
¼	Ovolo Tool	...	...	3/—	3/16	,, ,, 5 ,,		...	4/3
5/16	,, ,,	...	...	3/—	¼	,, ,, 2 ,,		...	1/9
3/8	,, ,,	...	...	3/—	¼	,, ,, 3 ,,		...	2/6
					¼	,, ,, 4 ,,		...	3/3
					¼	,, ,, 5 ,,		...	4/3

RECORD WORKS   -   -   SHEFFIELD, ENGLAND

C. & J. HAMPTON, LTD.   -   -   MANUFACTURERS

RECORD MULTI-PLANE, No. 405
SPECIAL BASES AND NOSING TOOL.

No. 10 Hollow.   No. 10 Round.

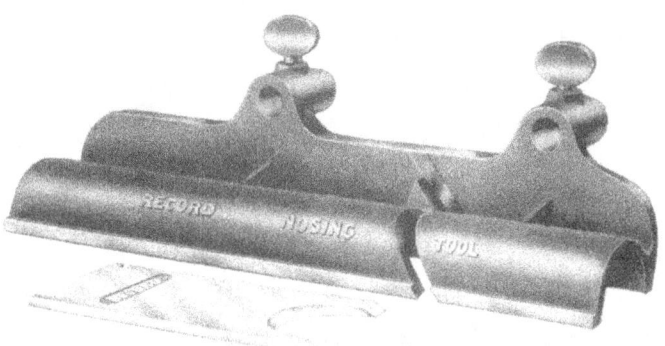

No. 5 Nosing Tool.

Special Bases are available for the Record Multi-Plane as illustrated above : a Hollow and its Cutter will form a Round ; a Round and its Cutter will form a Hollow.

A Nosing Tool and its Cutter will form a Round as, for example, in shaping the edges of stair treads.

Hollows and Rounds are sold in sets, comprising 1 Hollow, 1 Round and 2 Cutters.

No. and Type	Width of Cutter Inches	Works Circles Inches	Price per Set
No. 6 Hollow and Round	$\frac{1}{2}$	$\frac{3}{4}$	10/-
,, 8 ,, ,, ,,	$\frac{5}{8}$	1	10/-
,, 10 ,, ,, ,,	$\frac{3}{4}$	$1\frac{1}{4}$	11/-
,, 12 ,, ,, ,,	1	$1\frac{1}{2}$	11/-
,, 5 Nosing Tool	$1\frac{11}{16}$	$1\frac{1}{4}$	8/-
Extra CUTTERS for Hollows or Rounds ... 1/9 each			
Extra CUTTERS for Nosing Tool ... ... 2/- ,,			

RECORD WORKS   -   -   SHEFFIELD, ENGLAND

RECORD MULTI-PLANE

No. 405

The Record Multi-Plane will perform a wide range of cuts, including all those performed by the Combination Planes and the Plough Planes (see previous pages). The cross sections illustrated are suggestive of the cuts which can be made with the No. 405 Plane, using standard Cutters and also additional Cutters, and indicate in some instances the methods employed and the symbol letters and numbers of the Cutters used.

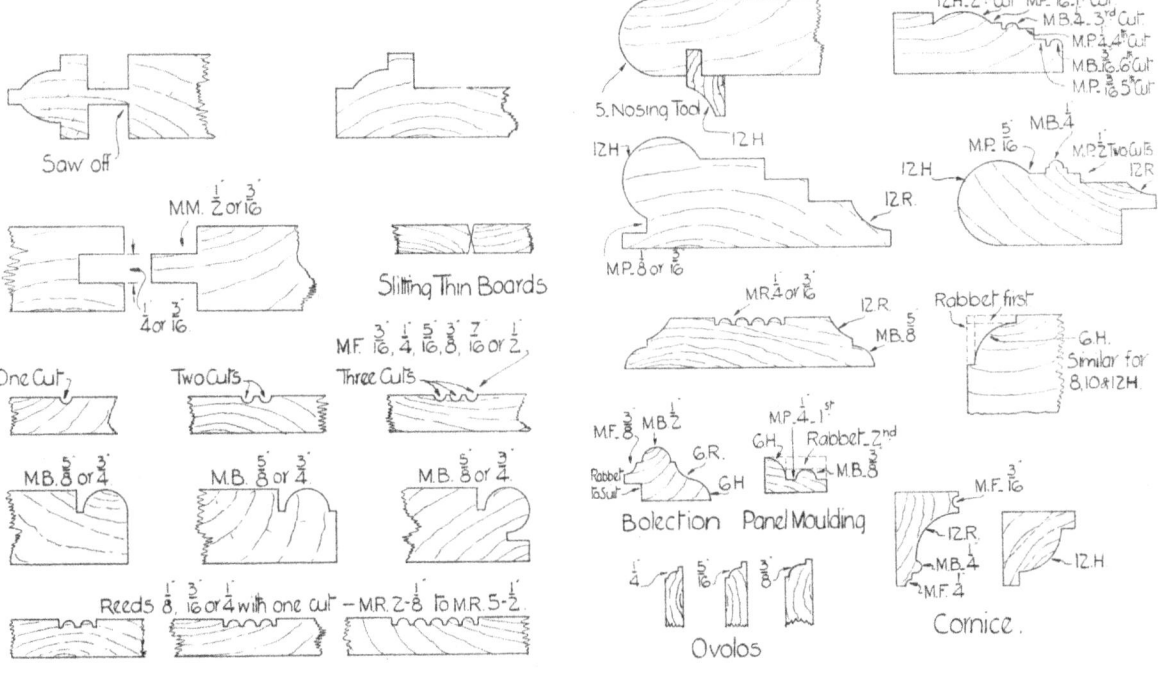

Continued on next page.

C. & J. HAMPTON, LTD. - - MANUFACTURERS

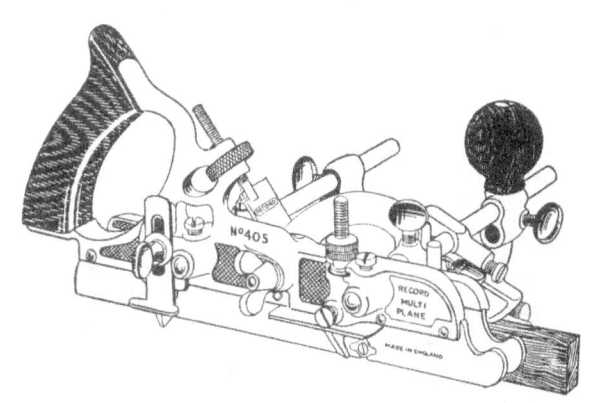

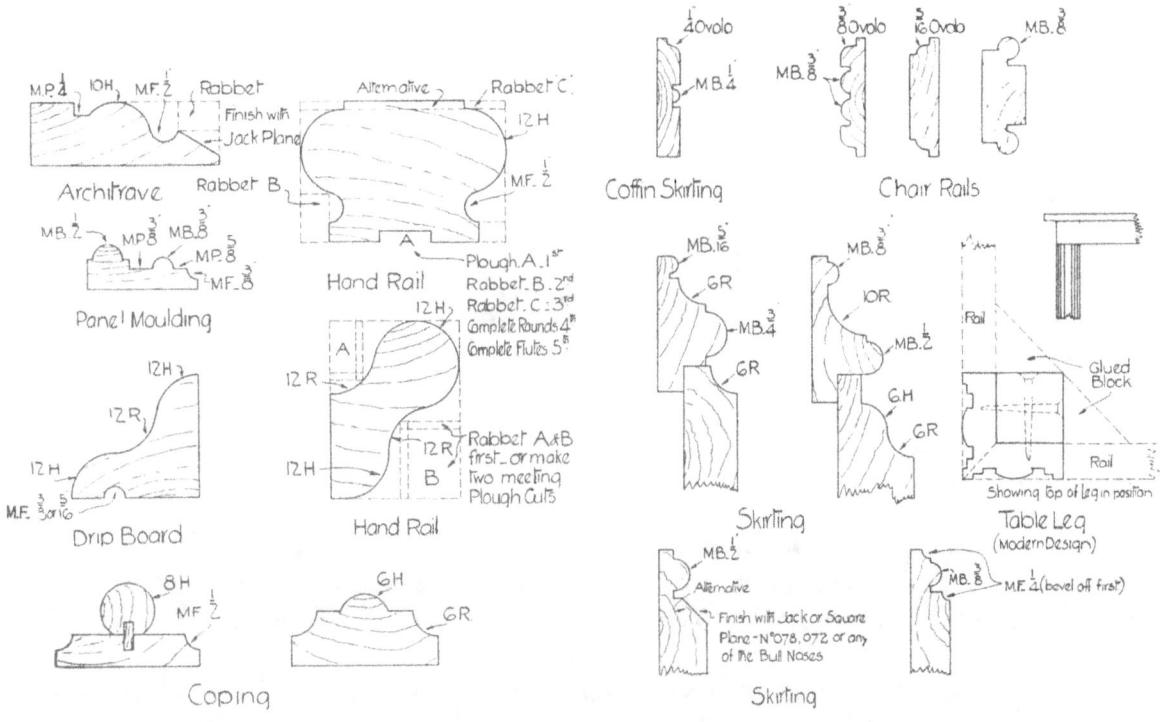

DADO CUTS, i.e., grooves across the grain, can also be performed with these Planes.

RECORD WORKS - - SHEFFIELD, ENGLAND

C. & J. HAMPTON, LTD. - - MANUFACTURERS

RECORD BLOCK PLANES

With TUNGSTEN STEEL Cutting Irons and ADJUSTABLE MOUTH.

The Base and Sides are ground and polished and there is a recess on each side for thumb and finger grip.

The Mouth is adjustable for fine or coarse work.

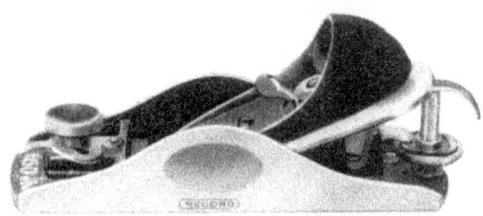

No. 09½ BLOCK PLANE.
6" long. 1⅝" Cutter. Weight 1½ pounds.
Code Word : Irday.
PRICE ... 8/– each.

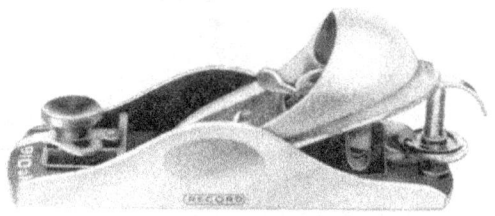

No. 016 BLOCK PLANE.
Nickel-plated Lever Cap.
6" long. 1⅝" Cutter. Weight 1½ pounds.
Code Word : Irdim.
PRICE ... 10/9 each.

No. 015 BLOCK PLANE.
7" long. 1⅝" Cutter. Weight 1⅝ pounds.
Code Word : Irdez.
PRICE ... 10/– each.

No. 017 BLOCK PLANE.
Nickel-plated Lever Cap.
7" long. 1⅝" Cutter. Weight 1⅝ pounds.
Code Word : Irdon.
PRICE ... 11/6 each.

These Planes are fitted with a Knuckle Joint Lever Cap which is made of Steel and is Nickel-plated. They have Screw Adjustment on the Cutter for regulating the depth of cut, and sidewise Adjustment is by Lever.

The Base and Sides are ground and polished, and there is a recess on each side for thumb and finger grip.

The Mouth is adjustable for fine or coarse work.

No. 018 BLOCK PLANE, Knuckle Joint. Adjustable.
6" long. 1⅝" Cutter. Weight 1½ pounds. Code Word : Irduo.
PRICE ... 11/6 each.

No. 019 BLOCK PLANE, Knuckle Joint. Adjustable.
7" long. 1⅝" Cutter. Weight 1⅝ pounds. Code Word : Irdyp.
PRICE ... 12/6 each.

Plane Irons and Plane Parts on pages 50 and 62.

All Planes packed 1 per box.

RECORD WORKS - - SHEFFIELD, ENGLAND

C. & J. HAMPTON, LTD.   -   -   MANUFACTURERS

RECORD BLOCK PLANES
With TUNGSTEN STEEL Cutting Irons.

The bases and sides are ground and polished, and a rosewood knob is fitted.

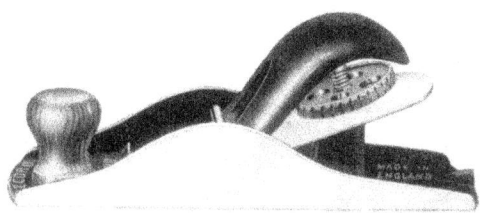

No. 0110 BLOCK PLANES.

Non-Adjustable.

No. 0110 Block Plane is non-adjustable. The Cutter is tightened in position by a nickel-plated knurled wheel and screw.

7" long.   1⅝" Cutter.   Weight 1⅜ pounds.
Code Word : Ipdau.
PRICE ... **4/–** each.

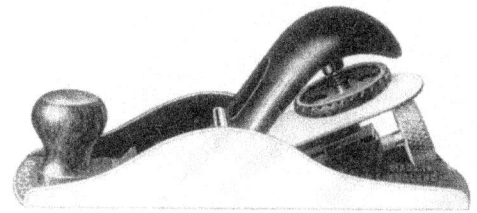

No. 0120 BLOCK PLANES.

Adjustable.

No. 0120 Block Plane has screw adjustment on the Cutter for regulating the depth of cut. The Cutter is tightened in position by a nickel-plated knurled wheel and screw.

7" long.   1⅝" Cutter.   Weight 1⅜ pounds.
Code Word : Ipdiz.
PRICE ... **5/6** each.

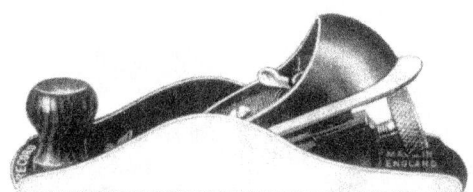

No. 0220 BLOCK PLANES.

Adjustable.

No. 0220 Block Plane has screw adjustment on the Cutter for regulating the depth of cut. The Cutter is tightened in position by a nickel-plated lever and cam.

7" long.   1⅝" Cutter.   Weight 1⅜ pounds.

Code Word : Ipdom.

PRICE ... **5/6** each.

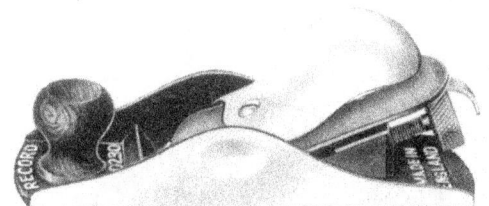

No. 0230 RECORD BLOCK PLANES, KNUCKLE JOINT.

Adjustable.

No. 0230 Plane is fitted with a Knuckle Joint Lever Cap which is made of steel and is nickel plated.

It has Screw Adjustment on the Cutter for regulating the depth of cut, and sidewise adjustment is by lever.

The base and sides are ground and polished, and there is a recess on each side for thumb and finger grip.

6" long.   1⅝" Cutter.   Weight 1 7/16 pounds.
Code Word : Ipdey.
PRICE ... **9/6** each.

Plane Irons and Plane Parts on pages 50, 51 and 63.

All Planes packed 1 per box.

RECORD WORKS   -   -   SHEFFIELD, ENGLAND

C. & J. HAMPTON, LTD. - - MANUFACTURERS

RECORD BLOCK PLANES
With TUNGSTEN STEEL Cutting Irons.

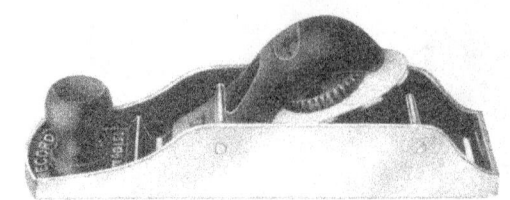

No. 0130 BLOCK PLANES. DOUBLE END.
Non-Adjustable.

No. 0130 Block Plane is non-adjustable. It has two mouths and illustration shows the Cutter in position for ordinary work. The Cutter and lever cap may be reversed to form a bull-nose plane.

The Cutter is tightened in either position by a nickel-plated knurled wheel and screw.

8" long.   1⅝" Cutter.   Weight 1⅝ pounds.

Code Word : Ipdun.

PRICE ... **6/-** each.

No. 0101 BLOCK PLANES
Non-Adjustable.

No. 0101 Block Plane is non-adjustable. The Cutter is tightened in position by a knurled screw.

3½" long.   1" Cutter.   Weight ¼ pound.

Code Word : Ipdyo.

PRICE ... **2/-** each.

No. 0102 RECORD BLOCK PLANES.
Non-Adjustable.

No. 0102 Block Plane is non-adjustable. The Cutter is tightened in position by a nickel-plated knurled wheel and screw. The base and sides are ground and polished.

5½" long.   1⅜" Cutter.   Weight ⅞ pound.

Code Word : Ipety.

PRICE ... **2/6** each.

Plane Irons and Plane Parts on pages 50, 51 and 63.

All Planes packed 1 per box.

RECORD WORKS - - SHEFFIELD, ENGLAND

C. & J. HAMPTON, LTD. - - MANUFACTURERS

RECORD ALL-STEEL SPOKE SHAVES
(Unbreakable)

No. A151
Steel Handles and Lever Caps.
Adjustable Cutter.
Raised Handle.
10" long. 2⅛" Cutter.
Weight 5 pounds per half-dozen.

No. A151. Flat Face. Code Word : Iposa.
PRICE ... **3/6** each.

No. A151R. Round Face. Code Word: Ipswa.
PRICE ... **3/6** each.

No. A51
Steel Handles and Lever Caps.
Double Iron.
The Cutter and Cap Iron are fastened by a thumbscrew, and adjustment can be made by releasing this screw.
Raised Handle.
10" long. 2⅛" Cutter.
Weight 4⅜ pounds per half-dozen.

No. A51. Flat Face. Code Word : Iporl.
PRICE ... **2/9** each.

No. A51R. Round Face. Code Word : Ipsil.
PRICE ... **2/9** each.

No. A63
Steel Handles and Lever Caps.
Straight Handle.
Light Double Iron.

No. A63. Round Face. Code Word : Ipoub.
9" long. 1¾" Cutter.
Weight 3 pounds per half-dozen.
PRICE ... **2/-** each.

No. A64
Steel Handles and Lever Caps.
Straight Handle.
Light Double Iron.

No. A64. Flat Face. Code Word : Ipowc.
9" long. 1¾" Cutter.
Weight 3 pounds per half-dozen.
PRICE ... **2/-** each.

Spoke Shave Irons on page 51.

Packed 6 per box.

RECORD WORKS - - SHEFFIELD, ENGLAND

C. & J. HAMPTON, LTD. -   -   MANUFACTURERS

RECORD SPOKE SHAVES
With TUNGSTEN STEEL Cutters.

No. 0151

Adjustable Cutter.
With Adjustable Cutter, Cap Iron and Raised Handle.

10″ long. $2\frac{1}{8}$″ Cutter.
Weight $4\frac{1}{4}$ pounds per half-dozen.

No. 0151.   Flat Face.   Code Word : Ippol.
PRICE   ...   2/9 each.

No. 0151R.   Round Face.   Code Word: Ippra.
PRICE   ...   2/9 each.

No. 0152

Adjustable Cutter.
With Adjustable Cutter, Cap Iron and Straight Handle.

10″ long. $2\frac{1}{8}$″ Cutter.
Weight $4\frac{1}{4}$ pounds per half-dozen.

No. 0152.   Flat Face.   Code Word : Ipsek.
PRICE   ...   2/9 each.

No. 0152R.   Round Face.   Code Word: Ipsyb.
PRICE   ...   2/9 each.

No. 051

Double Iron.
The Cutter and Cap Iron are fastened by a thumbscrew, and adjustment can be made by releasing this screw.

Raised Handle.
10″ long. $2\frac{1}{8}$″ Cutter.
Weight $4\frac{1}{8}$ pounds per half-dozen.

No. 051.   Flat Face.   Code Word : Ippaf.
PRICE   ...   2/- each.

No. 051R.   Round Face.   Code Word: Ippeg.
PRICE   ...   2/- each.

No. 052

Double Iron.
The Cutter and Cap Iron are fastened by a thumbscrew, and adjustment can be made by releasing this screw.

Straight Handle.
10″ long. $2\frac{1}{8}$″ Cutter.
Weight $4\frac{1}{8}$ pounds per half-dozen.

No. 052.   Flat Face.   Code Word : Ipreb.
PRICE   ...   2/3 each.

No. 052R.   Round Face.   Code Word : Iprue.
PRICE   ...   2/3 each.

Spoke Shave Irons on page 51.

Packed 6 per box.

RECORD WORKS   -   -   SHEFFIELD, ENGLAND

C. & J. HAMPTON, LTD.　-　-　MANUFACTURERS

RECORD SPOKE SHAVES

With TUNGSTEN STEEL Cutters.

No. 053

Adjustable Mouth.　Raised Handle.

The Mouth can be closed or opened for fine or coarse work.

No. 053.　Code Word : Ipphi.
10″ long.　2⅛″ Cutter.

Weight 4¼ pounds per half-dozen.

PRICE ... 2/6 each.

No. 055

Hollow Face.　Raised Handle.

No. 055.　Code Word : Ippik.
10″ long.　2⅛″ Cutter.

Weight 4 pounds per half-dozen.

PRICE ... 2/3 each.

No. 063

Round Face.　Straight Handle.
Light Double Iron.

No. 063.　Code Word : Ipoyd.
9″ long.　1¾″ Cutter.

Weight 2¾ pounds per half-dozen.

PRICE ... 1/6 each.

No. 064

Flat Face.　Straight Handle.
Light Double Iron.

No. 064.　Code Word : Ipoze.
9″ long.　1¾″ Cutter.

Weight 2¾ pounds per half-dozen.

PRICE ... 1/6 each.

Spoke Shave Irons on page 51.

Packed 6 per box.

RECORD WORKS　-　-　SHEFFIELD, ENGLAND

C. & J. HAMPTON, LTD. - - MANUFACTURERS

RECORD SCRAPERS

No. 080 Record Cabinet Scrapers.

Raised Double Handle.

The Scraping Iron is made to cut freely by springing it to a slight curve by the adjustment of the thumb screw.

The Iron has two scraping edges, and is reversible.

$11\frac{1}{2}"$ long. $2\frac{3}{4}"$ Cutter.   Weight $1\frac{1}{2}$ pounds.

Code Word : Iprod.

PRICE ... **4/6** each.

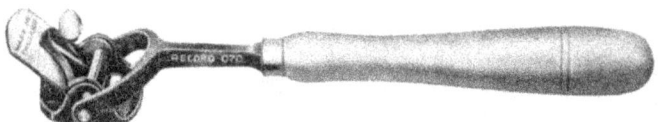

No. 070 Record Box Scrapers.

This Box Scraper is for scraping stencils and marks from the surface of boxes, floors, etc.

The Handle is hinged on the body, and the Cutter and bottom are slightly curved for scraping uneven surfaces. Ash Handle.

13" long.   2" Cutter.   Weight 1 pound.

Code Word : Ipryf.

PRICE ... **4/-** each.

Scraper Irons on page 51.

Packed 1 per box.

RECORD WORKS - - SHEFFIELD, ENGLAND

C. & J. HAMPTON, LTD. - - MANUFACTURERS

"PLANECRAFT"

136 Pages.   200 Illustrations and Diagrams.

Cloth Cover.   Size 9" x 6"

Price 1/6

TABLE OF CONTENTS:

Chapter	1	The History of the Plane	Chapter 9	Fundamentals of Planing
,,	2	The Bench Planes	,, 10	Rabbets and Rabbeting
,,	3	Adjustment of the Plane	,, 11	The Combination Plane, No. 050
,,	4	Grinding the Iron	,, 12	The Multi-Plane, No. 405
,,	5	Whetting the Iron	,, 13	The Circular Planes
,,	6	Holding the Bench Plane	,, 14	Router Planes
,,	7	Squaring up a piece of Wood	,, 15	Spoke Shaves
,,	8	Difficulties in Planing and their Solution	,, 16	Scrapers
			,, 17	The Bench Vice

Useful Glossary of Woodwork Terms

**A BOOK FULL OF INTERESTING AND HELPFUL INFORMATION.
A WORKSHOP COMPANION OF REAL SERVICE.**

"This book should be in the hands of every woodworker"
—vide Press.

RECORD WORKS - - SHEFFIELD, ENGLAND

C. & J. HAMPTON, LTD.   -   -   MANUFACTURERS

RECORD PLANE IRONS
(Tungsten Steel.)

The use of a Special Crucible Cast TUNGSTEN STEEL for Plane Irons or Cutters has been developed by the makers of Record Planes, and as a result of metallurgical research and exhaustive tests a quality of Steel has been produced which will retain its fine edge and fast cutting quality on the hardest woods.

Record Plane Irons are hardened and tempered under scientific control which ensures accuracy and uniformity. They are precision ground all over to ensure uniform thickness and parallelism which are so vital to the efficiency of the whole assembly and which eliminates the possibility of chatter or vibration.

THE REASON WHY RECORD PLANE IRONS CUT FASTER AND LAST LONGER.

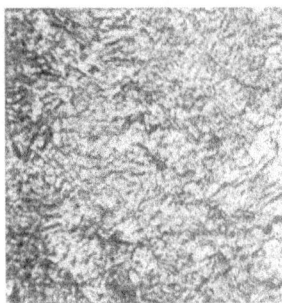
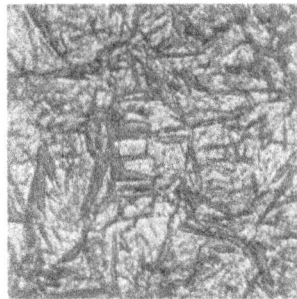

Views under microscope on same magnifications.

Tungsten Steel. Ordinary Cast Steel.

These photographs show the fineness of the grain of Tungsten Steel compared with that of ordinary Cast Steel.

This density means that Tungsten Steel is more resistant to wear and will take a keener cutting edge and hold it for a longer time than any other Steel.

Testing Record Plane Irons.

Every Record Plane Iron passes a final test on a Hardness Testing Machine and is guaranteed to be the right temper and correct in every way.

RECORD WORKS   -   -   SHEFFIELD, ENGLAND

C. & J. HAMPTON, LTD. - - MANUFACTURERS

RECORD PLANE IRONS

(TUNGSTEN STEEL).

Single Iron.

Double Iron.

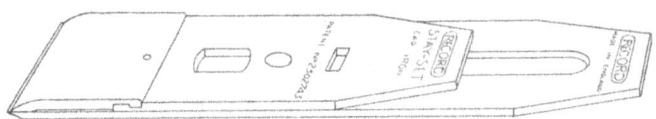

Cutter complete with STAY-SET Cap Iron and Screw.

For Plane No.	Type	Width of Cutter Inches	Single Cutter	Cutter, complete with Ordinary Cap Iron and Screw	Cutter, complete with STAY-SET Cap Iron and Screw	STAY-SET Cap Iron only
02	Smooth	1⅝	1/9	3/3	4/3	2/6
03	Smooth	1¾	2/3	3/9	4/9	2/6
04	Smooth	2	2/3	3/9	4/9	2/6
04½	Smooth	2⅜	2/9	4/3	5/3	2/6
05	Jack	2	2/3	3/9	4/9	2/6
05½	Jack	2¼	2/9	4/3	5/3	2/6
06	Fore	2⅜	2/9	4/3	5/3	2/6
07	Jointer	2⅜	2/9	4/3	5/3	2/6
08	Jointer	2⅝	2/9	4/3	5/3	2/6

All Spare Irons are interchangeable, and when ordering, Plane No. should be stated and exactly which type is required.

Plane Irons packed 6 per box.

Continued

RECORD WORKS - - SHEFFIELD, ENGLAND

C. & J. HAMPTON, LTD. - - MANUFACTURERS

RECORD PLANE IRONS
(TUNGSTEN STEEL).

For Plane No.	Type	Width of Cutter Inches	Price Each Single Cutter	Cutter, complete with Ordinary Cap Iron and Screw
010	Rabbet	$2\frac{1}{8}$	2/6	4/–
010$\frac{1}{2}$	Rabbet	$2\frac{1}{8}$	2/6	4/–
020	Circular	$1\frac{3}{4}$	2/3	3/9
0113	Circular	$1\frac{3}{4}$	2/3	3/9
040	Plough	See page 26		
043	Plough	See page 26		
044	Plough	See page 28		
050A	Combination	See page 31		
405	Multi-Plane	See pages 35 & 36		
071	Router	$\frac{1}{4}$	2/6	
071	Router	$\frac{1}{2}$	2/6	
071	Router	Smoothing Cutter	2/6	
071$\frac{1}{2}$	Router	$\frac{1}{4}$	2/6	
071$\frac{1}{2}$	Router	$\frac{1}{2}$	2/6	
071$\frac{1}{2}$	Router	Smoothing Cutter	2/6	
722	Router	$\frac{1}{4}$	1/3	
041	Shoulder Rabbet	$\frac{5}{8}$	1/6	
042	Shoulder Rabbet	$\frac{3}{4}$	1/9	
072	Shoulder Rabbet	1	2/–	
073	Shoulder Rabbet	$1\frac{1}{4}$	2/3	
074	Shoulder Rabbet	$1\frac{1}{2}$	2/6	
075	Bull-Nose Rabbet	1	1/6	
076	Bull-Nose Rabbet	$1\frac{1}{8}$	1/6	
077	Bull-Nose Rabbet	$1\frac{1}{8}$	1/9	
077A	Bull-Nose Rabbet	$1\frac{1}{8}$	1/9	
311	"Three-in-One"	$1\frac{1}{8}$	1/9	
1366	Bull-Nose Rabbet	$\frac{3}{8}$	1/6	
2506	Side Rabbet	$\frac{1}{2}$	1/9	(pair)
2506S	Side Rabbet	$\frac{1}{2}$	1/9	(,,)
078	Duplex Rabbet	$1\frac{1}{2}$	1/9	
09$\frac{1}{2}$	Block	$1\frac{5}{8}$	1/6	
015	Block	$1\frac{5}{8}$	1/6	
016	Block	$1\frac{5}{8}$	1/6	
017	Block	$1\frac{5}{8}$	1/6	
018	Block	$1\frac{5}{8}$	1/6	
019	Block	$1\frac{5}{8}$	1/6	
0101	Block	$1\frac{3}{8}$	8d.	
0102	Block	$1\frac{3}{8}$	1/–	
0110	Block	$1\frac{5}{8}$	1/3	

RECORD WORKS - - SHEFFIELD, ENGLAND

C. & J. HAMPTON, LTD.   -   -   MANUFACTURERS

RECORD PLANE IRONS
Continued

For Plane No.	Type	Width of Cutter Inches	Price Each	
			Single Cutter	Cutter, complete with Ordinary Cap Iron and Screw
0120	Block...	1⅝	1/6	
0130	Block...	1⅝	1/3	
0220	Block...	1⅝	1/6	
0230	Block...	1⅝	1/6	
400½	Scrub...	1½	2/3	
712	Skew Rabbet ...	1¼	1/9	
713	Skew Rabbet ...	1½	2/-	
714	Skew Rabbet ...	1¾	2/3	

SPARE IRONS for RECORD SPOKE SHAVES and SCRAPERS

	Width of Cutter Inches	Price Each
For Spoke Shave No.		
051	2⅛	10d.
052	2⅛	10d.
053	2⅛	10d.
055	2⅛	10d.
063	1¾	8d.
064	1¾	8d.
0151	2⅛	10d.
0152	2⅛	10d.
A51	2⅛	10d.
A63	1¾	8d.
A64	1¾	8d.
A151	2⅛	10d.
For Scraper No.		
070	2	1/-
080 Plain	2¾	1/3
080 Coarse Tooth	2¾	2/6
080 Fine Tooth	2¾	2/6

RECORD WORKS   -   -   SHEFFIELD, ENGLAND

HINTS FOR GRINDING AND HONING PLANE IRONS

The best results are only obtained when the Cutting Iron Bevel is ground at the correct angle, which is 25 degrees, and a line gauge for this purpose is stamped on the Cap Iron and should be used as shown below. Water should be used on the grindstone wherever possible to prevent the temper of the Iron being drawn and a square should be used to ensure that the cutting edge is ground square with the sides of the Iron.

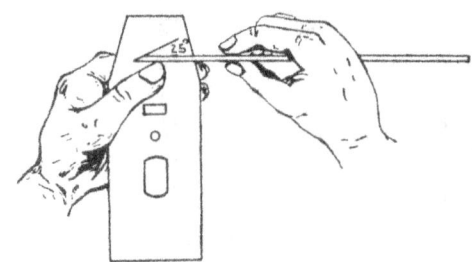

The process of honing or whetting is simply rubbing the bevelled edge of the Iron on the face of the oilstone. The best kind of stone for Plane Irons (and also for Chisels and other carpenters' tools) is a medium cutting grit which may be either natural or artificial, i.e., manufactured. With natural stones, there is still an element of luck as to whether one secures a good one, but if a well-known brand is procured, such as the Lillywhite Washita, it is possible to get a good one.

Of the manufactured stones, the India stone will serve well, and a two-sided one, i.e., medium and fine, will give good service. For a really keen edge that is a delight to use, the edge should be finished off on an Arkansas stone. If the stone is new it should be soaked in oil for a few days (India stones excepted, for they are oil-filled already).

First put a few drops of oil on the stone and wipe it thoroughly clean with a rag —not shavings, which are apt to fill the pores of the stone with dust and grit. Having cleaned the stone and put a few drops of oil on it, bring Iron into contact with the stone. Feel the bevel in contact throughout and then raise the back slightly so that you will work on the front, i.e., the cutting edge. The best motion is "to and fro," though some craftsmen use a figure of 8 motion.

Use as much of the flat surface of the stone as possible, for in this way the wear on the stone is more evenly spread. Do not allow the iron to "rock," as this must inevitably result in a curved edge that cannot cut well and will necessitate re-grinding straight away. Keep the wrists rigid and the angle of iron to stone constant. Apply a moderate pressure and keep whetting until the line of reflected light on the edge disappears.

There will be a certain amount of wire edge rubbed away, and this will hang on at the extreme edge. To remove it, turn the Iron over absolutely flat on the stone and give two or three light rubs. On no account have the Iron raised so that this produces a bevel.

An ultra keen edge can be obtained by finishing off on a leather strop placed flat on the bench. The strop should be dressed with Russian tallow and a little fine flour emery.

C. & J. HAMPTON, LTD.   -   -   MANUFACTURERS

RECORD BRASS PLUMB BOBS
No. 1405.

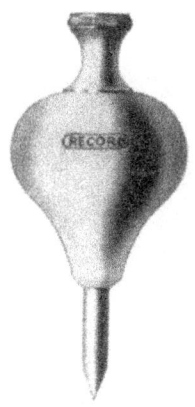

Polished and Lacquered.

Record Plumb Bobs are made with Steel Points and removable threaded Cap for inserting the line.

The weights given are approximate.

Code Word : Iparz.

Approx. Weight oz.	1½	2½	3	4½	6	8	10	13	16
No.	00	0	01	2	3	4	5	6	6½
Price Dozen	12/-	15/-	18/-	24/-	30/-	36/-	42/-	54/-	66/-

Packed 6 per box.

RECORD WORKS   -   -   SHEFFIELD, ENGLAND

C. & J. HAMPTON, LTD.   -   -   MANUFACTURERS

PARTS for RECORD ADJUSTABLE IRON PLANES

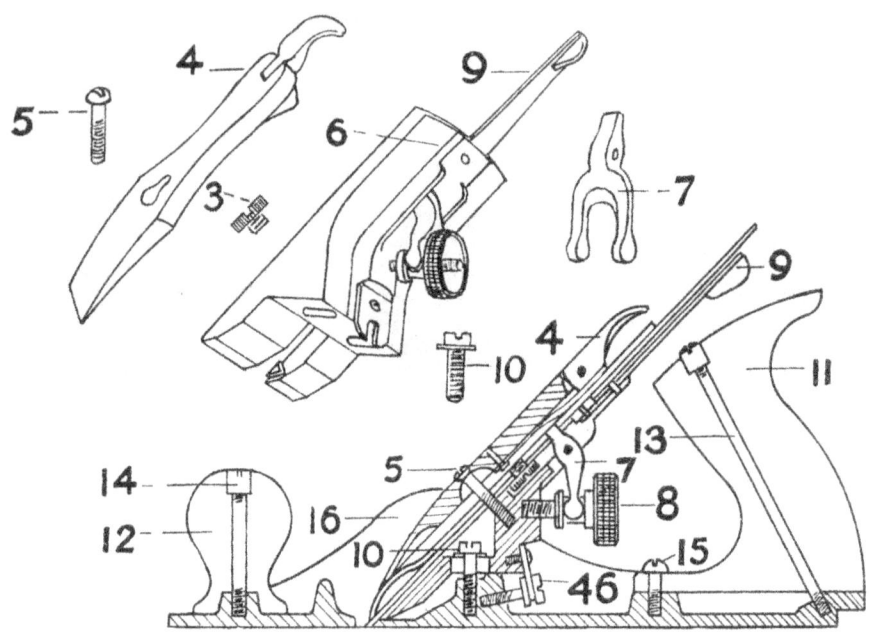

Ref. No. on Diagram	Name of Part	For Plane No.										
		02	03	04	04½	05	05½	06	07	08	010	010½
3	Cap Screw	6d.	6d.	6d.	6d.	6d.	6d.	6d.	6d.	6d.	6d.	6d.
4	Lever Cap	2/–	2/–	2/–	2/–	2/–	2/–	2/–	2/–	2/–	2/–	2/–
5	Lever Cap Screw	6d.	6d.	6d.	6d.	6d.	6d.	6d.	6d.	6d.	6d.	6d.
6	Frog, complete	3/–	3/–	3/–	3/–	3/–	3/–	3/–	3/–	3/–	3/–	3/–
7	"Y" Adjusting Lever	6d.	6d.	6d.	6d.	6d.	6d.	6d.	6d.	6d.	6d.	6d.
8	Adjusting Nut	9d.	9d.	9d.	9d.	9d.	9d.	9d.	9d.	9d.	9d.	9d.
9	Lateral Adjusting Lever	9d.	9d.	9d.	9d.	9d.	9d.	9d.	9d.	9d.	9d.	9d.
10	Frog Screw	6d.	6d.	6d.	6d.	6d.	6d.	6d.	6d.	6d.	6d.	6d.
11	Plane Handle	1/9	1/9	1/9	1/9	1/9	1/9	1/9	1/9	1/9	1/9	1/9
12	Plane Knob	1/3	1/3	1/3	1/3	1/3	1/3	1/3	1/3	1/3	1/3	1/3
13	Handle Bolt and Nut	9d.	9d.	9d.	9d.	9d.	9d.	9d.	9d.	9d.	9d.	9d.
14	Knob Bolt and Nut	9d.	9d.	9d.	9d.	9d.	9d.	9d.	9d.	9d.	9d.	9d.
15	Handle Toe Screw	—	—	—	6d.	6d.	6d.	6d.	6d.	6d.	—	—
16	Plane Body	8/3	8/3	8/3	10/–	10/–	10/–	13/9	19/6	23/9	13/9	13/9
46	Frog Adjusting Screw	6d.	6d.	6d.	6d.	6d.	6d.	6d.	6d.	6d.	6d.	6d.

RECORD WORKS   -   -   SHEFFIELD, ENGLAND

C. & J. HAMPTON, LTD. - - MANUFACTURERS

PARTS for RECORD DUPLEX RABBET and FILLETSTER PLANE
No. 078

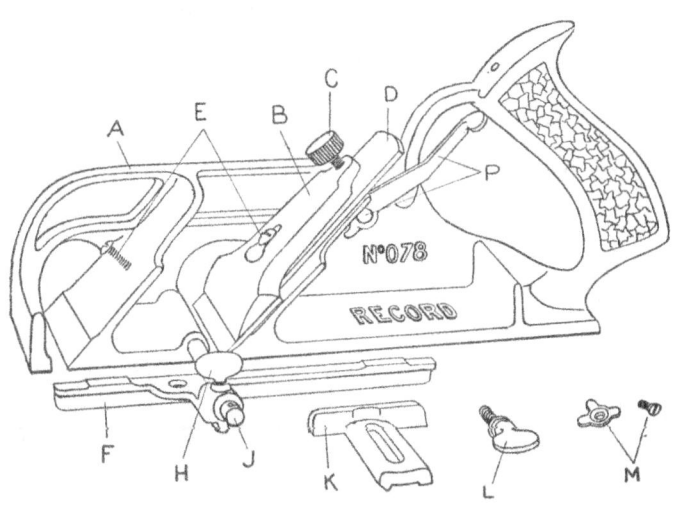

A.	Body	8/3
B.	Lever Cap	9d.
C.	Lever Cap Knurled Screw	6d.
D.	Cutting Iron	1/9
E.	Lever Cap Screw	6d.
F.	Fence	2/-
H.	Fence Thumbscrew	6d.
J.	Fence Arm	9d.
K.	Adjusting Depth Gauge	1/-
L.	Adjusting Depth Gauge Thumbscrew and Washer	6d.
M.	Spur and Screw	6d.
P.	Adjusting Lever and Rivet	9d.

RECORD WORKS - - SHEFFIELD, ENGLAND

C. & J. HAMPTON, LTD. - - MANUFACTURERS

PARTS for RECORD BULL-NOSE RABBET PLANES

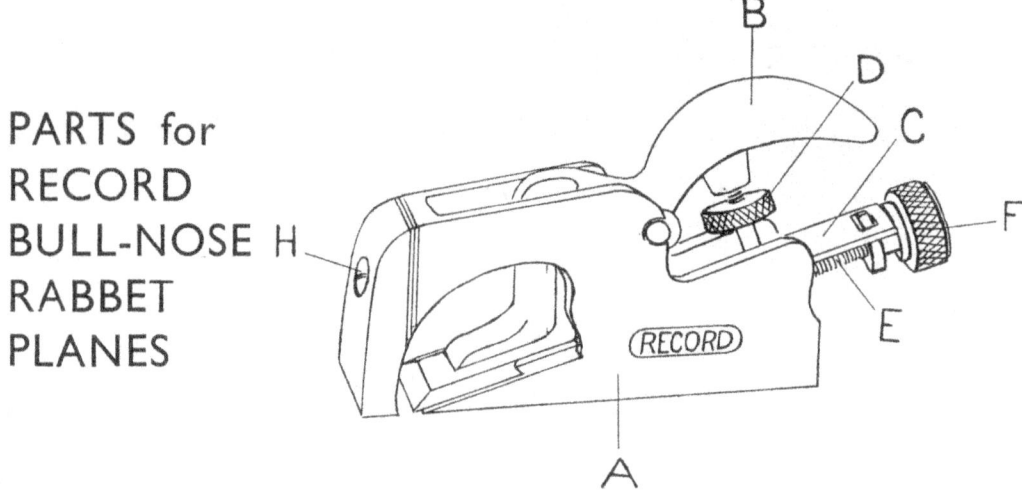

	For Plane No.	076	077	077A	311
A.	Body (complete with Nose, Distance Pieces and Screw on No. 077A)	4/6	8/–	9/–	9/–
B.	Lever Cap	1/9	3/–	3/–	3/–
C.	Cutting Iron	1/6	1/9	1/9	1/9
D.	Lever Cap Screw	6d.	6d.	6d.	6d.
E.	Cutting Iron Adjusting Screw	—	6d.	6d.	6d.
F.	Cutting Iron Adjusting Screw Nut	—	9d.	9d.	9d.
H.	Nose Locking Screw	—	—	3d.	3d.

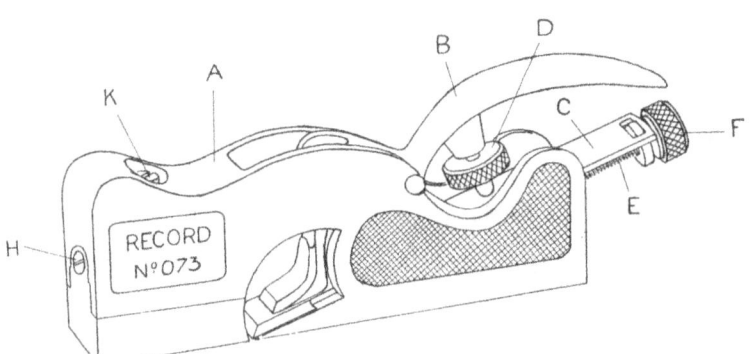

PARTS for RECORD IMPROVED SHOULDER RABBET PLANES

	For Plane No.	041	042	072	073	074
A.	Body (complete with Adjustable Mouth Slide and Screws on Nos. 072, 073 and 074)	8/–	12/–	18/6	20/6	22/6
B.	Lever Cap	3/–	3/6	6/6	7/6	8/6
C.	Cutting Iron	1/6	1/9	2/–	2/3	2/6
D.	Lever Cap Screw	9d.	9d.	9d.	9d.	9d.
E.	Iron Adjusting Screw	6d.	6d.	6d.	6d.	6d.
F.	Iron Adjusting Screw Nut	9d.	9d.	9d.	9d.	9d.
H.	Mouth Adjusting Screw	—	—	3d.	3d.	3d.
K.	Mouth Locking Screw and Washer	—	—	9d.	9d.	9d.

RECORD WORKS - - SHEFFIELD, ENGLAND

C. & J. HAMPTON, LTD. - - MANUFACTURERS

PARTS for
RECORD SKEW RABBET PLANES

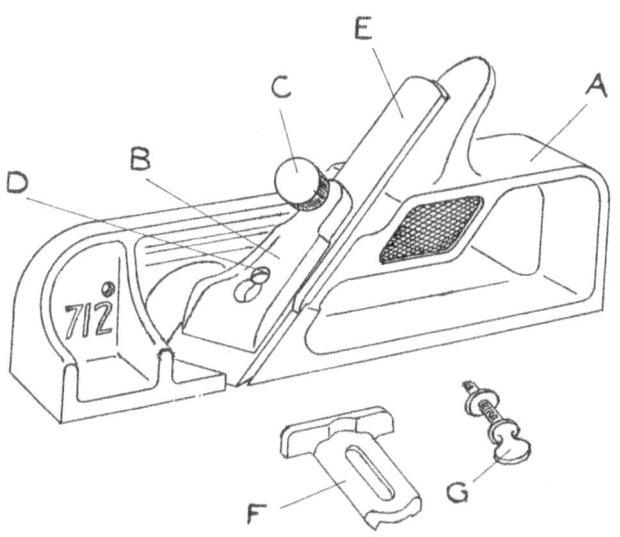

		For Plane No.	712	713	714
A.	Body		5/3	5/9	6/3
B.	Lever Cap		9d.	9d.	9d.
C.	Lever Cap Knurled Screw		6d.	6d.	6d.
D.	Lever Cap Screw		6d.	6d.	6d.
E.	Cutting Iron		1/9	2/-	2/3
F.	Adjusting Depth Gauge		1/-	1/-	1/-
G.	Adjusting Depth Gauge Thumbscrew and Washer		6d.	6d.	6d.

RECORD WORKS - - SHEFFIELD, ENGLAND

C. & J. HAMPTON, LTD.   -   -   MANUFACTURERS

PARTS for RECORD ROUTER PLANES

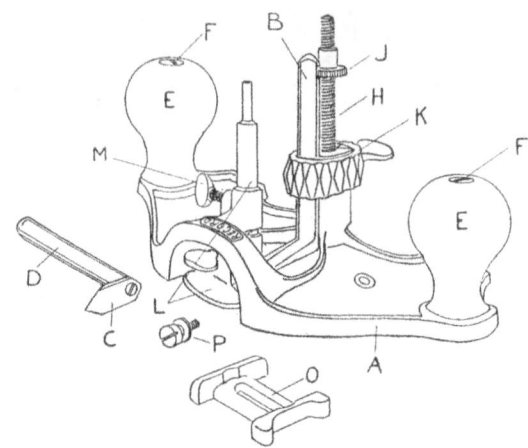

	For Plane No.	071	071½
A.	Body ...	8/3	7/-
B.	Plane Irons ... each	2/6	2/6
E.	Knobs ... ,,	1/3	1/3
F.	Knob Bolt and Nut ... ,,	9d.	9d.
H.	Cutter Adjusting Screw ...	6d.	6d.
J.	Cutter Adjusting Nut ...	9d.	9d.
K.	Cutter Clamping Collar and Thumbscrew ...	2/-	2/-
L.	Depth Gauge and Shoe ...	2/-	—
O.	Fence, Screw and Washer ...	1/-	1/-

PARTS for RECORD CIRCULAR PLANES

	For Plane No.	020	0113
Double Iron ...		3/9	3/9
Single Iron ...		2/3	2/3
Lever Cap ...		2/-	2/-
Lever Cap Screw ...		6d.	6d.
Frog, complete ...		3/-	3/-
Frog Seat ...		4/-	—
Frame Casting ...		12/6	8/6
Plane Bottom, complete with Fittings ...		5/-	6/-
Bottom Adjusting Screw ...		2/-	4/-
Bottom Adjusting Screw Nut ...		2/-	—
Segment Plates and Spindles ... per set		—	3/-

RECORD WORKS   -   -   SHEFFIELD, ENGLAND

C. & J. HAMPTON, LTD. - - MANUFACTURERS

PARTS for RECORD PLOUGH PLANES

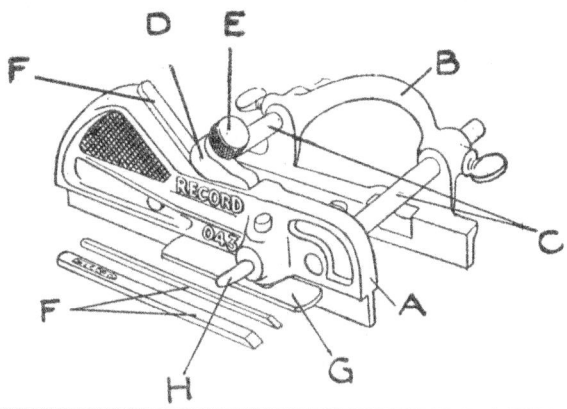

		For Plane No.	040	043
A.	Main Stock		4/-	6/-
B.	Fence		1/9	2/9
C.	Arm Rod		9d.	—
C.	Arm Rods ... per pair		—	1/6
D.	Lever Cap		6d.	9d.
E.	Lever Cap Knurled Screw		6d.	6d.
F.	Cutters ... per set of 3		2/9	2/9
G.	Depth Gauge		1/6	1/6
H.	Depth Gauge Locking Screw		6d.	6d.

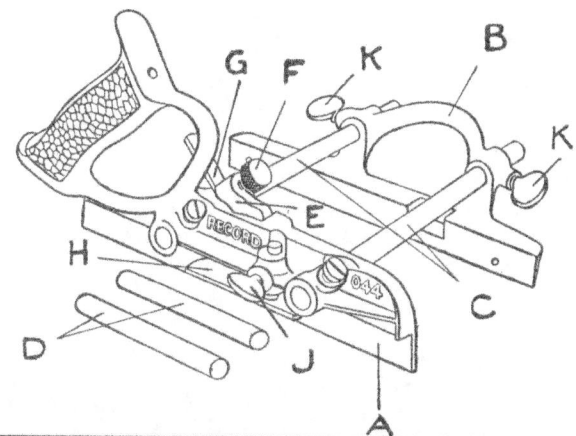

		For Plane No.	044
A.	Main Stock		9/-
B.	Fence		4/-
C.	Long Arms ... per pair		2/-
D.	Short Arms ... "		1/-
E.	Lever Cap		9d.
F.	Lever Cap Knurled Screw		6d.
G.	Cutters ... per set of 8		8/6
H.	Depth Gauge		1/6
J.	Depth Gauge Locking Screw		6d.
K.	Fence Locking Screws ... each		6d.

RECORD WORKS - - SHEFFIELD, ENGLAND

C. & J. HAMPTON, LTD. - - MANUFACTURERS

PARTS for RECORD COMBINATION PLANES, Nos. 050 and 050A

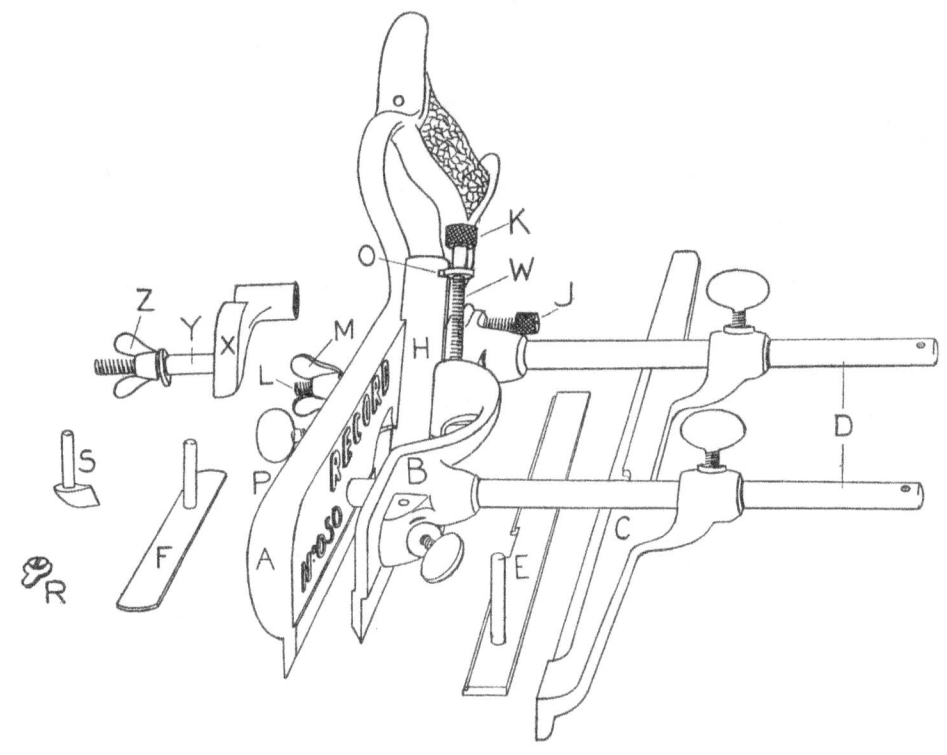

A.	Main Stock	10/6
B.	Sliding Section	6/6
C.	Fence	4/-
D.	Arm Rods ... per pair	2/6
E.	Beading Stop	2/6
F.	Depth Gauge	1/6
H.	Cutters ... per set of 15	14/6
J.	Sliding Section Fixing Screw	9d.
K.	Cutter Adjusting Nut	6d.
L.	Cutter Bolt	9d.
M.	Cutter Bolt Wing Nut	6d.
R.	Spurs, with screws (set, 2 pairs)	1/-
S.	Shaving Deflector	9d.
W.	Iron Adjusting Screw	9d.
X.	Cutter Clamping Bracket	2/-
Y.	Cutter Clamping Bracket Bolt	9d.
Z.	Cutter Clamping Bracket Washer and Wing Nut	6d.

RECORD WORKS - - SHEFFIELD, ENGLAND

C. & J. HAMPTON, LTD.   -   -   MANUFACTURERS

PARTS for RECORD MULTI-PLANE, No. 405

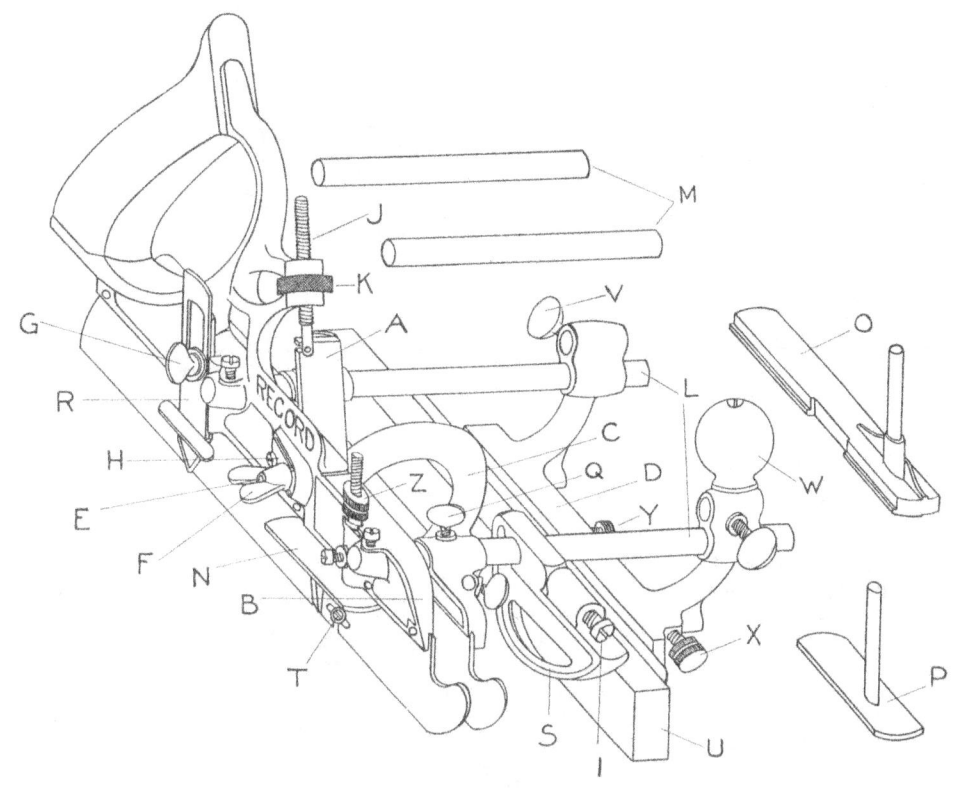

A.	Standard Cutters ... ...Complete set of 23	29/-
B.	Main Stock	21/-
C.	Sliding Section	12/6
D.	Fence (complete)	6/3
E.	Cutter Bolt	1/3
F.	Cutter Bolt Wing Nut	1/3
H.	Cutter Bolt Clip and Screw	6d.
J.	Cutter Adjusting Screw	9d.
K.	Cutter Adjusting Screw Wheel	9d.
L.	Long Arms ... ... pair	4/-
M.	Short Arms ... ... ,,	2/-
N.	Adjustable Depth Gauge	1/9
O.	Adjustable Beading Stop	1/9
P.	Sliding Section Depth Gauge	1/9
R.	Slitting Cutter Stop	9d.
S.	Cam Steady	3/3
T.	Spurs and Screws	6d.
W.	Knob and Bolt and Nut	2/-

RECORD WORKS   -   -   SHEFFIELD, ENGLAND

C. & J. HAMPTON, LTD. - - MANUFACTURERS

PARTS for RECORD BLOCK PLANES

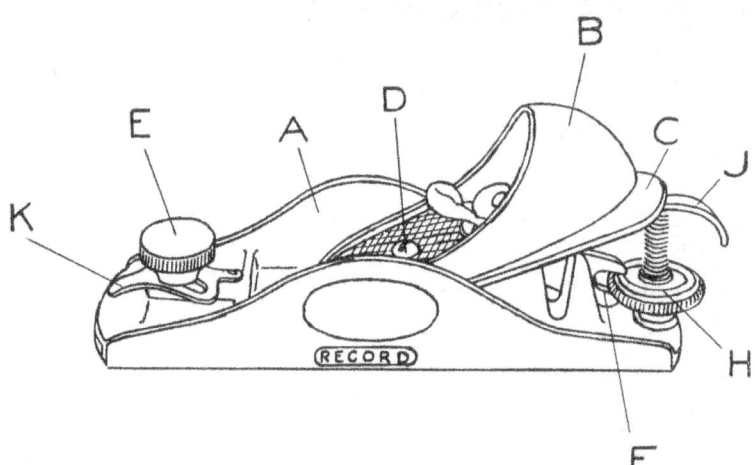

	For Plane No.	09½	015	016	017
A.	Body complete with Adjustable Mouth Plate.	5/9	6/3	6/3	6/3
B.	Lever Cap	9d.	9d.	1/3	1/3
C.	Cutting Iron	1/6	1/6	1/6	1/6
D.	Lever Cap Screw	6d.	6d.	6d.	6d.
E.	Front Knob	9d.	9d.	9d.	9d.
F.	Cutting Iron Adjusting Lever	6d.	6d.	6d.	6d.
H.	Adjusting Nut	9d.	9d.	9d.	9d.
J.	Lateral Adjusting Lever	9d.	9d.	9d.	9d.
K.	Adjustable Mouth Cam Lever	9d.	9d.	9d.	9d.

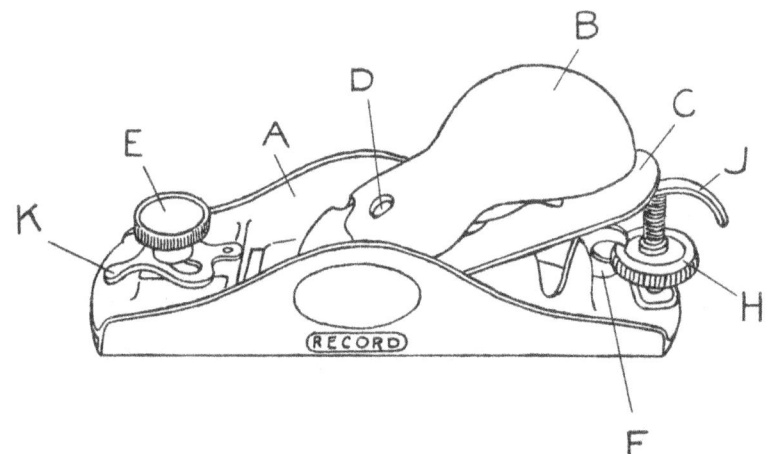

	For Plane No.	018	019
A.	Body complete with Adjustable Mouth Plate	6/3	6/3
B.	Lever Cap	4/6	4/6
C.	Cutting Iron	1/6	1/6
D.	Lever Cap Screw	6d.	6d.
E.	Front Knob	9d.	9d.
F.	Cutting Iron Adjusting Lever	6d.	6d.
H.	Adjusting Nut	9d.	9d.
J.	Lateral Adjusting Lever	9d.	9d.
K.	Adjustable Mouth Cam Lever	9d.	9d.

RECORD WORKS - - SHEFFIELD, ENGLAND

C. & J. HAMPTON, LTD. - - MANUFACTURERS

PARTS for RECORD BLOCK PLANES

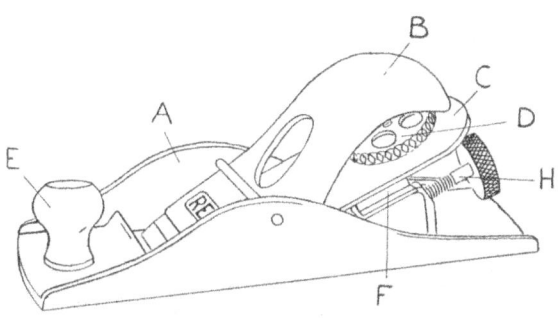

		For Plane No.	0101	0102	0110	0120	0130
A.	Body		1/3	1/9	2/-	2/6	4/6
B.	Lever Cap		6d.	9d.	9d.	9d.	9d.
C.	Cutting Iron		8d.	1/-	1/3	1/6	1/3
D.	Lever Cap Tightening Screw		3d.	4d.	4d.	4d.	4d.
E.	Knob		—	—	9d.	9d.	9d.
F.	Frog Slide		—	—	—	1/-	—
H.	Frog Slide Adjusting Screw		—	—	—	1/3	—

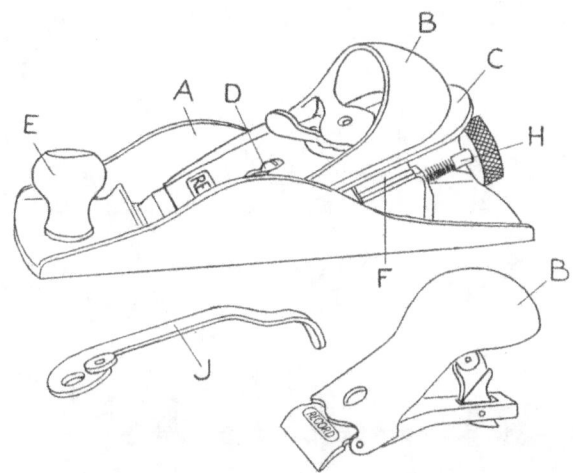

		For Plane No.	0220	0230
A.	Body		2/6	3/-
B.	Lever Cap		9d.	4/6
C.	Cutting Iron		1/6	1/6
D.	Lever Cap Screw		6d.	6d.
E.	Knob		9d.	9d.
F.	Frog Slide		1/-	1/-
H.	Frog Slide Adjusting Screw		1/3	1/3
J.	Lateral Adjusting Lever		—	9d.

RECORD WORKS - - SHEFFIELD, ENGLAND

C. & J. HAMPTON, LTD. - - MANUFACTURERS

DISPLAY STAND for RECORD PLANES

This Display Stand is supplied free with stock order for Planes.

RECORD WORKS - - SHEFFIELD, ENGLAND

HAND & BREAST DRILLS
Pages 66-76

SECTION 2

C. & J. HAMPTON, LTD.   -   -   MANUFACTURERS

RECORD HAND DRILLS, No. 122

CHUCK.—3-Jaw All-Steel Chuck with hardened Steel Jaws and protected Springs. Nickel-plated finish.

GEARS.—Single speed. Ball-thrust Bearing. Machine-cut Gears throughout. Steel Pinion and Gear Spindle.

HANDLE.—Solid Hardwood Handle, Rosewood finish.

FRAME.—Malleable Iron Frame.

FINISH.—Finished Dark Blue with Red Gear Wheel. Other parts Nickel-plated.

Capacity 0 to $\frac{1}{4}''$ round shank Drills.

Length $12\frac{1}{2}''$.   Weight $1\frac{1}{2}$ pounds.   Code Word : Ilvom.

PRICE (without Twist Drills), **8/-** each.

Packed 1 per box.

RECORD WORKS   -   -   SHEFFIELD, ENGLAND

C. & J. HAMPTON, LTD. - - MANUFACTURERS

RECORD HAND DRILLS, No. 123

CHUCK.—3-Jaw All-Steel Chuck with hardened Steel Jaws and protected Springs. Nickel-plated finish.

GEARS.—Single speed. Ball-thrust Bearing. Machine-cut Gears throughout. Steel Pinions and Spindles. Double Pinion including Idler Pinion.

HANDLE.—Hollow Hardwood. This handle will take full-length Jobbers' Twist Drills.

FRAME.—Malleable Iron Frame.

FINISH.—Finished Dark Blue with Red Gear Wheel. Other parts Nickel-plated.

Capacity 0 to $\frac{1}{4}''$ round shank Drills.

Length $14\frac{1}{4}''$.   Weight $1\frac{1}{2}$ pounds.

No. 123ND (without Twist Drills).   Code Word : Ilvyo.

PRICE **9/6** each.

No. 123, with 7 Carbon Steel Twist Drills.   Code Word : Ilvun.

PRICE **11/6** each.

Packed 1 per box.

RECORD WORKS - - SHEFFIELD, ENGLAND

C. & J. HAMPTON, LTD. - - MANUFACTURERS

RECORD IMPROVED HAND DRILLS, No. 124

CHUCK.—3-Jaw All-Steel Chuck with hardened Steel Jaws and protected Springs. Nickel-plated finish.

GEARS.—Single speed. Ball-thrust Bearing. Machine-cut Gears throughout. Steel Pinions and Spindles. Double Pinion including Idler Pinion to equalize the bearings. Large Gear with wide knurled rim.

HANDLE.—Hollow Hardwood. This handle will take full-length Jobbers' Twist Drills.

FRAME.—Malleable Iron Frame with improved gripping lug.

FINISH.—Finished Dark Blue with Red Gear Wheel, Nickel-plated on rim. Other parts Nickel-plated.

All the knobs are made of Bakelite of a beautiful mahogany colour and fine finish, and are more durable than wood.

Capacity 0 to $\frac{1}{4}''$ round shank Drills.

Length $14\frac{1}{4}''$.   Weight (approx.) 2 pounds.   Code Word : Ilwap.

PRICE (without Twist Drills), **12/6** each.

Packed 1 per box.

RECORD WORKS - - SHEFFIELD, ENGLAND

C. & J. HAMPTON, LTD. - - MANUFACTURERS

RECORD IMPROVED HAND DRILLS, No. 125

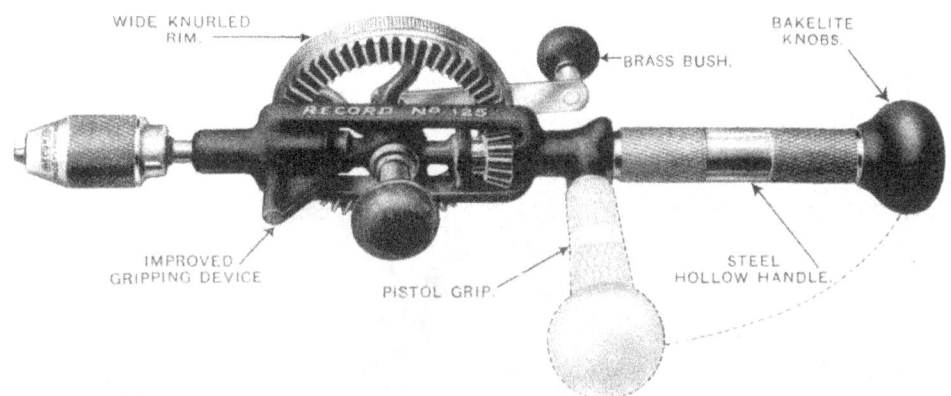

CHUCK.—3-Jaw All-Steel Chuck with hardened Steel Jaws and protected Springs. Nickel-plated finish.

GEARS.—Single speed. Ball-thrust Bearing. Machine-cut Gears throughout. Steel Pinions and Spindles. Double Pinion, including Idler Pinion to equalize bearings. Large Gear with wide knurled rim.

HANDLE.—Nickel-plated Hollow Steel Handle. This handle will take full-length Jobbers' Twist Drills.

FRAME.—Malleable Iron Frame with improved gripping lug.

FINISH.—Finished Dark Blue with Red Gear Wheel, Nickel-plated on rim. Other parts Nickel-plated.

All the knobs are made of Bakelite of a beautiful mahogany colour and fine finish, and are more durable than wood.

Capacity 0 to $\frac{1}{4}''$ round shank Drills.

Length $13\frac{3}{4}''$. Weight (approx.) 2 pounds.

No. 125ND (without Twist Drills). Code Word : Ilwis.

PRICE **14/-** each.

No. 125, with 7 Carbon Steel Twist Drills. $\frac{1}{16}''$ to $\frac{1}{4}''$. Code Word : Ilwer.

PRICE **16/-** each.

Packed 1 per box.

RECORD WORKS - - SHEFFIELD, ENGLAND

C. & J. HAMPTON, LTD. - - MANUFACTURERS

RECORD BREAST DRILLS
No. 144

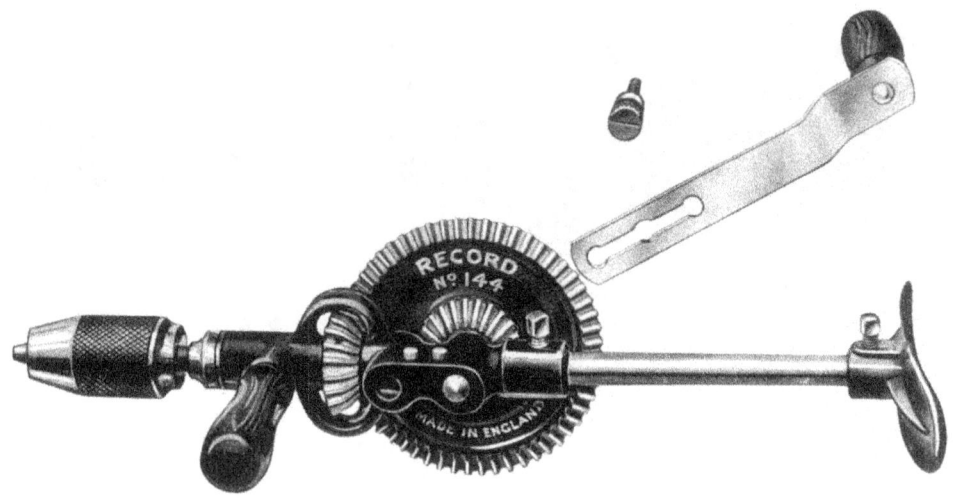

CHUCK.—3-Jaw All-Steel Chuck with hardened Steel Jaws and protected Springs. Nickel-plated finish.

SPEED.—Two. Press plunger for quick change.

GEARS.—Machine-cut throughout. Steel Pinion.

BODY.—Cast Iron Body. Steel Shank. Ball-thrust Bearing. Adjustable Breast Plate.

HANDLES.—Stained Hardwood. The Crank Handle is extensible from 4" to 6" radius.

Capacity 0 to ½" round shanks.

Length 17". Weight 5¾ pounds. Code Word : Ilyem.
PRICE 16/- each.

No. 144MC. As above but fitted with Master 2-Jaw Chuck. Code Word : Ilzas.
PRICE 18/- each.

Packed 1 per box.

RECORD WORKS - - SHEFFIELD, ENGLAND

C. & J. HAMPTON, LTD. - - MANUFACTURERS

RECORD BREAST DRILLS, No. 145

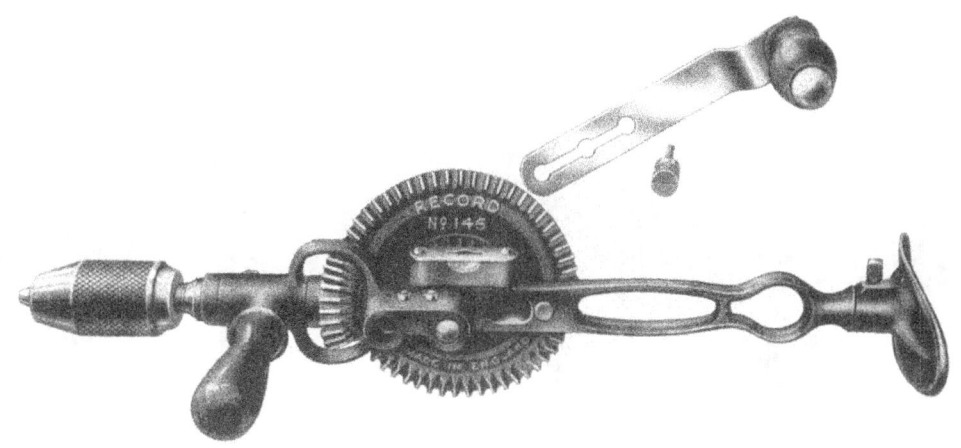

CHUCK.—3-Jaw All-Steel Chuck with hardened Steel Jaws and protected Springs. Nickel-plated finish.

SPEED.—Two. Press plunger for quick change.

GEARS.—Machine-cut throughout. Steel Pinion. Idler Roll to equalize bearing.

BODY.—Malleable Iron Body. Annular Ball-bearing Spindle. Ball-thrust Bearing. Adjustable Breast Plate. Spirit Level attached.

HANDLES.—Solid Hardwood. The Crank Handle is extensible from 4″ to 6″ radius.

Capacity 0 to $\frac{1}{2}$″ round shanks.

Length 18″. Weight 6 pounds. Code Word : Ilymo.

PRICE **22/6** each.

Packed 1 per box.

RECORD WORKS - - SHEFFIELD, ENGLAND

C. & J. HAMPTON, LTD. - - MANUFACTURERS

RECORD BREAST DRILLS, No. 146

CHUCK.—Master 2-Jaw All-Steel Chuck with hardened Steel Jaws. Nickel-plated finish.

SPEED.—Two. Press plunger for quick change.

GEARS.—Machine-cut throughout. Steel Pinion. Idler Roll to equalize bearing.

BODY.—Malleable Iron Body. Annular Ball-bearing Spindle. Ball-thrust Bearing. Adjustable Breast Plate. Spirit Level attached.

HANDLES.—Solid Hardwood. The Crank Handle is extensible from 4″ to 6″ radius.

Capacity $\frac{1}{8}$″ to $\frac{1}{2}$″ round shanks, bit stock shanks and No. 1 Morse taper shanks.

Length 18″. Weight 6 pounds. Code Word : Ilyur.

PRICE **24/6** each.

Packed 1 per box.

RECORD WORKS - - SHEFFIELD, ENGLAND

C. & J. HAMPTON, LTD. - - MANUFACTURERS

RECORD DRILL CHUCKS

Record Drill Chucks are made entirely of Steel. They are fitted with three hardened and ground Steel Jaws, which are controlled by concealed Springs and are protected from damage in use. Nickel-plated finish.

Capacity Diameter	Type	Chuck No.	Price Each	Code Word
0" to 1/4"	Chuck with Straight Shank, 2½" x ½" dia.	322S	4/-	Ilhag
	Chuck with No. I Morse Taper Shank	322T	4/9	Ilhei
	Chuck with Bit Brace Shank	322B	5/9	Ilhik
0" to 3/8"	Chuck with Straight Shank, 2½" x ½" dia.	326S	5/6	Iljaf
	Chuck with No. I Morse Taper Shank	326T	6/3	Iljeg
	Chuck with Bit Brace Shank	326B	7/3	Iljoi
0" to ½"	Chuck with Straight Shank, 2½" x ½" dia.	345S	7/-	Ilkea
	Chuck with No. I Morse Taper Shank	345T	7/6	Ilkib
	Chuck with Bit Brace Shank	345B	8/6	Ilkud

Chucks packed 1 per box.

RECORD WORKS - - SHEFFIELD, ENGLAND

C. & J. HAMPTON, LTD.   -   -   MANUFACTURERS

PARTS for RECORD HAND DRILLS

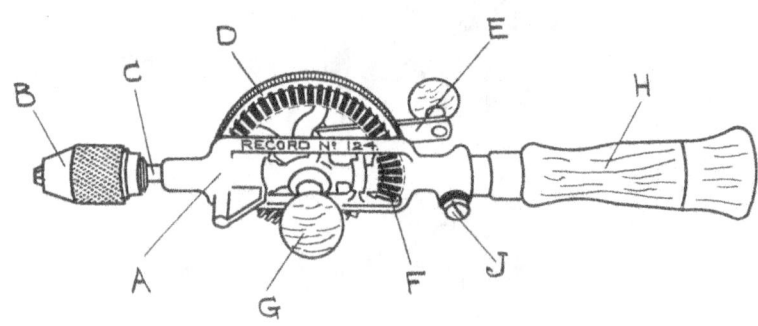

	For Drill No.	122	123	124	125
A	Frame	1/6	1/9	2/-	2/-
B	Chuck	3/-	3/-	3/-	3/-
C	Spindle for Chuck	9d.	9d.	9d.	9d.
D	Large Gear Wheel	2/6	2/6	3/3	3/3
E	Crank Handle with Knob	9d.	9d.	1/-	1/-
F	Crown Wheels	9d. each	1/9 pair	1/9 pair	1/9 pair
G	Side Knob	9d.	9d.	1/-	1/-
H	Handle	9d.	1/-	1/-	2/6
J	Locking Screw for Handle	...	...	6d.	6d.
—	Small Screw for Crank Handle	3d.	3d.	3d.	3d.
—	Large ,, ,,	6d.	6d.	6d.	6d.

RECORD WORKS   -   -   SHEFFIELD, ENGLAND

C. & J. HAMPTON, LTD.   -   -   MANUFACTURERS

PARTS for RECORD BREAST DRILLS

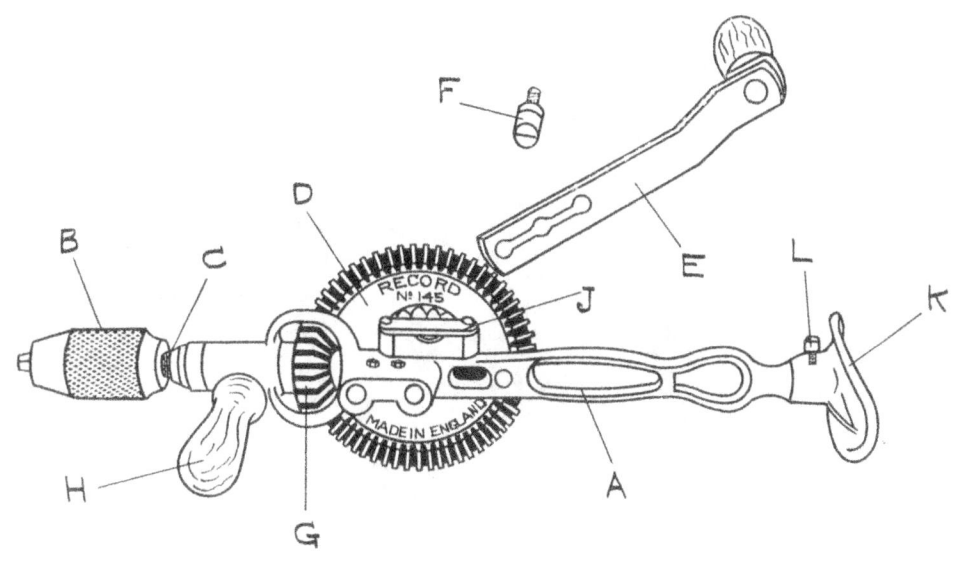

		For Drill No.	144	145	146
A	Frame		3/6	4/6	4/6
B	Chuck (No. 146 complete with Spindle)		5/–	5/–	8/6
C	Spindle for Chuck		1/6	1/6	...
D	Large Gear Wheel		5/6	5/6	5/6
E	Crank Handle		2/3	2/3	2/3
F	Screw for Fixing Crank Handle		1/–	1/–	1/–
G	Crown Wheel		2/9	2/9	2/9
H	Side Handle		9d.	9d.	9d.
J	Spirit Level		...	1/9	1/9
K	Breast Plate		2/3	3/–	3/–
L	Screw for Breast Plate		9d.	9d.	9d.
—	Screw for Steel Shank		9d.	...	...

RECORD WORKS   -   -   SHEFFIELD, ENGLAND

C. & J. HAMPTON, LTD.   -   -   MANUFACTURERS

RECORD DRILL DISPLAY No. 10

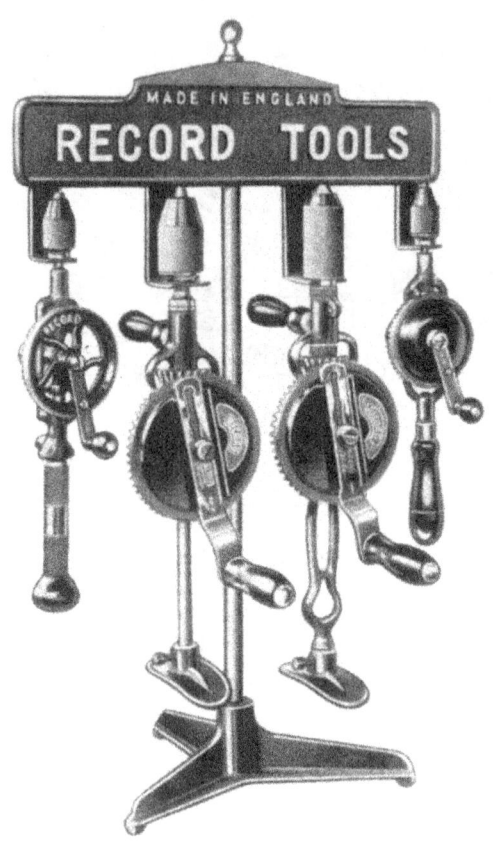

The Record Drill Display Stand shown above is supplied FREE with an order comprising 10 Drills as specified below:

    2 No. 122   Record Hand Drills
    2 No. 123ND   ,,   ,,   ,,
    2 No. 124   ,,   ,,   ,,
    1 No. 125   ,,   ,,   ,,
    2 No. 144   ,,   Breast   ,,
    1 No. 145   ,,   ,,   ,,

RECORD WORKS   -   -   SHEFFIELD, ENGLAND

SECTION 3

VICES for Metal and Wood
Pages 78-118

C. & J. HAMPTON, LTD.   -   -   MANUFACTURERS

RECORD MECHANICS' VICES

With Patent Unbreakable Nut.

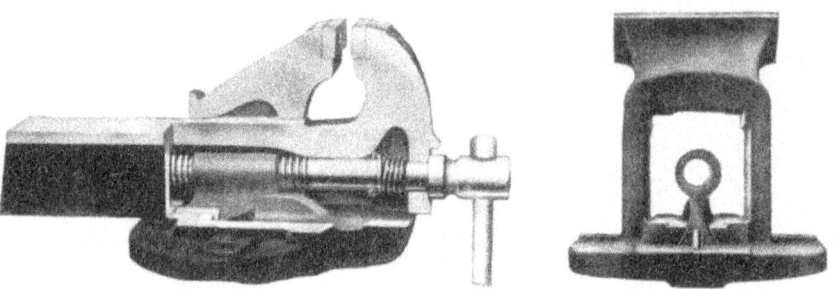

Registered Design No. 666,598.
Patent No. 196,858.

Record Mechanics' Vices are the most popular plain screw Vices of modern times due to their exclusive features of strength and reliability. The design was developed from long experience in the manufacture of Vices, and is the outcome of actual breaking tests made until all weaknesses were eliminated.

They are fitted with a Patent Unbreakable Solid Nut, which is recognised as the greatest improvement made in parallel Vices for a number of years past, and is an exclusive feature of Record Vices.

This Nut brings the Record Mechanics' Vice up to a machine tool standard, wherein the vital wearing parts are made for long service and to be renewable should it ever be necessary.

Security and rigidity are essential with a detachable Nut, and as the "Record" Nut is dovetailed into the base of the Body, it is absolutely fixed and rigid in the Vice. The front of the Nut faces up to a strong abutment, which takes all the pressure close up underneath the screw.

This method of securing the Nut in the vice body, together with the long barrel of the Nut (which is equal to three diameters of the screw), ensures perfect alignment of the Screw and Nut under the greatest pressure.

The Body and Sliding Jaw are Cast Iron of guaranteed strength.

The Steel Jaw Plates of Record Vices are renewable and interchangeable. They can be supplied with Smooth Faces if desired.

RECORD WORKS   -   -   SHEFFIELD, ENGLAND

C. & J. HAMPTON, LTD.   -   -   MANUFACTURERS

RECORD MECHANICS' VICES

With Patent Unbreakable Nut.

Stationary Base.   Plain Screw Type.

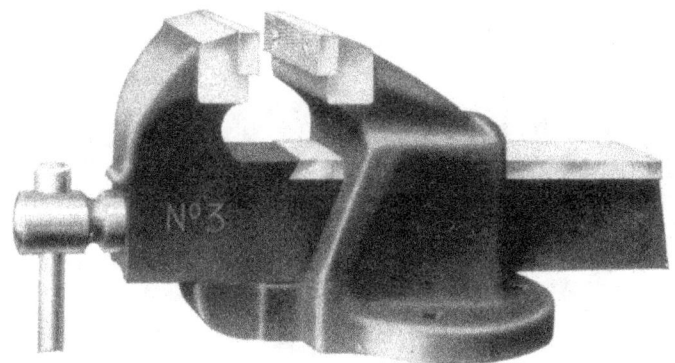

Registered Design No. 666,598.
Patent No. 196,858.

Vice No.	Width of Jaws Inches	List Price Each	Opening Inches	Depth of Jaws Inches	Approx. Weight Pounds	Code Word
00	2¼	10/6	2¼	1½	5½	Ibcob
0	2½	12/-	2½	1⅝	8	Ibafa
1	3	14/6	3¼	1⅞	12	Ibbab
2	3½	19/6	4	2⅜	21	Ibbec
3	4	25/-	4¾	2¾	33	Ibbid
4	4½	33/-	5½	3	42	Ibboe
5	5	41/-	6½	3¼	54	Ibbuf
6	6	55/-	8	3½	72	Ibbyg
7	7	65/-	9¼	4	84	Ibcai
8	8	72/-	9¼	4	90	Ibcek

RECORD WORKS   -   -   SHEFFIELD, ENGLAND

C. & J. HAMPTON, LTD. - - MANUFACTURERS

SWIVEL BASES for RECORD MECHANICS' VICES

Patent No. 125,707.

Record Patent Swivel Bases are of simple construction, having only two working parts, viz., the base ring and the inner swivelling disc.

These Swivel Bases enable Vices to be swivelled in a complete circle and firmly locked at any point by the two tightening levers.

This method of swivelling to suit the convenience of working is now more generally recognised and appreciated by Vice Users.

For Vice No. ...	00	0	1	2	3	4	5	6	7	8
LIST PRICE ...	5/6	6/-	7/-	9/6	13/6	15/-	19/-	20/-	20/-	20/-

RECORD WORKS - - SHEFFIELD, ENGLAND

C. & J. HAMPTON, LTD. - - MANUFACTURERS

RECORD MECHANICS' VICES

With Patent Unbreakable Nut.

With Swivel Base.   Plain Screw Type.

Registered Design No. 666,598.
Patents No. 196,858 and 125,707.

Vice No.	Width of Jaws Inches	List Price Each	Opening Inches	Depth of Jaws Inches	Approx. Weight Pounds	Code Word
00S	$2\frac{1}{4}$	16/-	$2\frac{1}{4}$	$1\frac{1}{2}$	7	Ibnuz
0S	$2\frac{1}{2}$	18/-	$2\frac{1}{2}$	$1\frac{5}{8}$	$9\frac{1}{2}$	Ibmam
1S	3	21/6	$3\frac{1}{4}$	$1\frac{7}{8}$	14	Ibmen
2S	$3\frac{1}{2}$	29/-	4	$2\frac{3}{8}$	25	Ibmio
3S	4	38/6	$4\frac{3}{4}$	$2\frac{3}{4}$	38	Ibmop
4S	$4\frac{1}{2}$	48/-	$5\frac{1}{2}$	3	46	Ibmur
5S	5	60/-	$6\frac{1}{2}$	$3\frac{1}{4}$	65	Ibmys
6S	6	75/-	8	$3\frac{1}{2}$	87	Ibnat
7S	7	85/-	$9\frac{1}{4}$	4	97	Ibniu
8S	8	92/-	$9\frac{1}{4}$	4	100	Ibnoy

RECORD WORKS - - SHEFFIELD, ENGLAND

C. & J. HAMPTON, LTD.   -   -   MANUFACTURERS

RECORD FITTERS' VICES

Stationary Base.   Quick-Grip Type.

Record Fitters' Vices combine quick-grip with screw-all-the-way action.

By depressing the trigger on to the screw head the jaws can be opened or closed instantaneously. This quick action saves considerable time.

The Body and Sliding Jaw are Cast Iron of guaranteed strength.

The Steel Jaw Plates are renewable and interchangeable.

Vice No.	Width of Jaws Inches	List Price Each	Opening Inches	Depth of Jaws Inches	Approx. Weight Pounds	Code Word
21	$3\frac{1}{4}$	34/-	4	$2\frac{3}{8}$	33	Icalb
22	$3\frac{3}{4}$	41/-	5	$3\frac{1}{8}$	47	Icanc
23	$4\frac{1}{4}$	49/-	6	$3\frac{3}{8}$	62	Icard
24	$5\frac{1}{4}$	60/-	7	$3\frac{7}{8}$	80	Icase
25	6	71/-	8	$4\frac{1}{2}$	95	Icawf
27	7	90/-	9	5	112	Icbek
28	8	135/-	10	$5\frac{7}{8}$	185	Icbil

RECORD WORKS   -   -   SHEFFIELD, ENGLAND

C. & J. HAMPTON, LTD. - - MANUFACTURERS

RECORD FITTERS' VICES

With Swivel Base.   Quick-Grip Type.

Swivel Base Patent No. 125,707.

These Vices can be swivelled in a complete circle and firmly locked at any point by the two tightening levers.

Vice No.	Width of Jaws Inches	List Price Each	Opening Inches	Depth of Jaws Inches	Approx. Weight Pounds	Code Word
21S	$3\frac{1}{4}$	44/–	4	$2\frac{3}{8}$	44	Idarb
22S	$3\frac{3}{4}$	52/–	5	$3\frac{1}{8}$	60	Idasc
23S	$4\frac{1}{4}$	61/–	6	$3\frac{3}{8}$	75	Idawd
24S	$5\frac{1}{4}$	75/–	7	$3\frac{7}{8}$	95	Idaxe
25S	6	88/–	8	$4\frac{1}{2}$	112	Idayf
27S	7	110/–	9	5	130	Idbik

RECORD WORKS - - SHEFFIELD, ENGLAND

C. & J. HAMPTON, LTD. - - MANUFACTURERS

RECORD AUTO VICE
No. 74

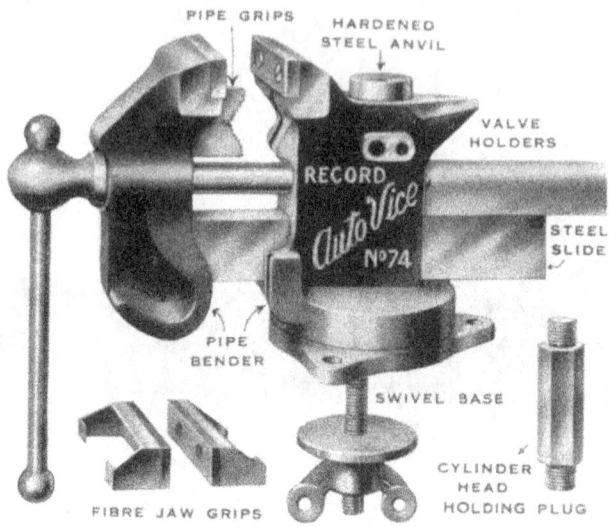

Patent No. 310,723 and Abroad.

SPECIAL FEATURES.

1. Swivel Base enables the Vice to be swivelled and firmly locked at any point for convenience of working.
2. Off-set Jaws to admit long and wide work vertically.
3. Hardened Steel Anvil.
4. Pipe Grips with hardened Steel Jaw.
5. Pipe and Rod Bender.
6. Steel Plug (screwed English and American plug threads) for holding cylinder heads of motor engines.
7. Detachable Steel Clam Jaws, faced with special Fibre to prevent damage when gripping Engine Parts, etc.

SPECIFICATION.

Width of Jaws 4".   Opening $4\frac{1}{2}$".
Pipe Jaws will take up to $1\frac{1}{2}$" outside diameter.
Approximate Weight 26 pounds.   Code Word : Iltum.
PRICE **32/6** each.

Packed complete in box.

RECORD WORKS - - SHEFFIELD, ENGLAND

C. & J. HAMPTON, LTD.   -   -   MANUFACTURERS

RECORD ALL-STEEL GARAGE VICE
No. 75

For Heavy Duty.   **Unbreakable.**

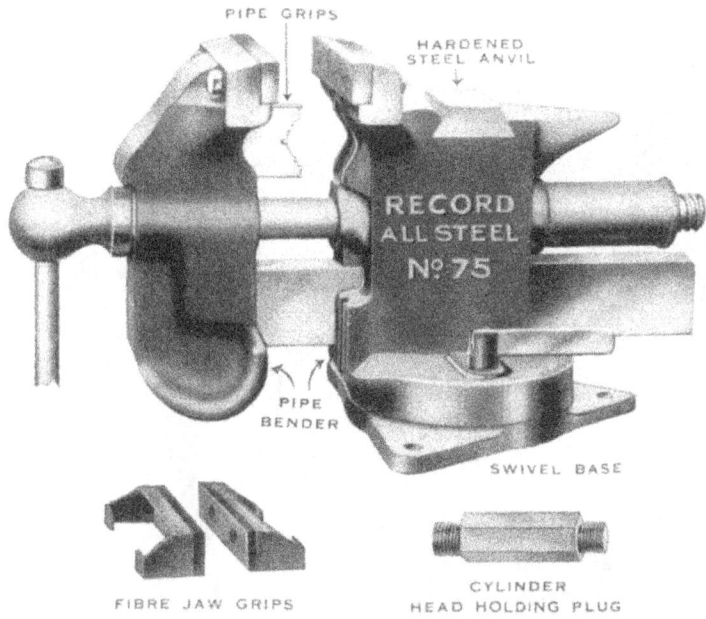

Patent No. 310,723 and Abroad.

SPECIAL FEATURES.

1. Swivel Base enables the Vice to be swivelled and firmly locked at any point for convenience of working.
2. Off-set Jaws to admit long and wide work vertically.
3. Hardened Steel Anvil.
4. Pipe Grips with hardened Steel Jaw.
5. Pipe and Rod Bender.
6. Steel Plug (screwed English and American plug threads) for holding cylinder heads of motor engines.
7. Detachable Steel Clam Jaws, faced with special Fibre to prevent damage when gripping Engine Parts, etc.

SPECIFICATION.

Width of Jaws $5\frac{1}{4}''$.   Extra wide opening $7''$.
Pipe Jaws will take up to $2\frac{3}{4}''$ outside diameter.
Approximate Weight 48 pounds.   Code Word : Iltyn.

PRICE **75/-** each.

Packed complete in box.

RECORD WORKS   -   -   SHEFFIELD, ENGLAND

C. & J. HAMPTON, LTD. - - MANUFACTURERS

RECORD FOLDING TRIPOD STAND
No. 574

Complete with Record Auto Vice.

Enlarged illustration of Vice showing Special Features.

Portable, compact and convenient for taking to the work.
The Record Auto Vice No. 74 incorporates the following SPECIAL FEATURES
(as fully described on page 84).

1. Swivel Base.
2. Off-set Jaws.
3. Hardened Steel Anvil.
4. Pipe Grips.
5. Pipe and Rod Bender.
6. Valve Holders.
7. Cylinder Head Holding Plug.
8. Detachable Fibre Jaw Grips.

	List Price Each Complete	Approx. Weight Pounds	Code Word
No. 574 Stand, complete with a No. 74 RECORD Auto Vice, 4" width of Jaws, 4½" opening, Pipe Jaws will take up to 1½" outside diameter.	59/6	72	Idgel

RECORD WORKS - - SHEFFIELD, ENGLAND

C. & J. HAMPTON, LTD.   -   -   MANUFACTURERS

RECORD "IMP" TABLE VICE
No. 80

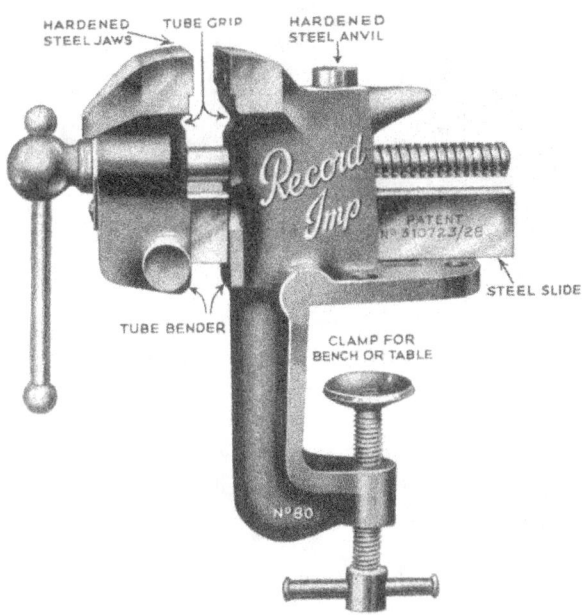

Patent No. 310,723.

A sturdy and compact Vice for general use on bench or table.

It will also grip small tubes and bend rods, and has Hardened Steel Jaws and Anvil, Steel Slide, and machine-cut square thread Screw.

Width of Jaws $2\frac{1}{4}$".   Opening $2\frac{1}{2}$".

Weight $4\frac{1}{4}$ pounds.   Code Word : Impib.

PRICE **10/-** each.

Packed in box.

RECORD WORKS   -   -   SHEFFIELD, ENGLAND

C. & J. HAMPTON, LTD. - - MANUFACTURERS

RECORD STEEL VICES

Guaranteed Unbreakable. Stationary Base.

Registered Design No. 666,598.

Record Steel Vices are specially recommended for Filers and Fitters. They are made of Steel throughout and are unbreakable in use. There is ample clearance beneath the jaws to allow irregular-shaped articles to be gripped.

The Jaw Plates are secured by screws having fine threads and long taper heads to ensure rigidity, and are renewable and interchangeable.

QUICK-GRIP TYPE.

Vice No.	Width of Jaws Inches	List Price Each	Opening Inches	Depth of Jaws Inches	Approx. Weight Pounds	Code Word
34	4½	72/–	5	3	35	Ifate
35	5¼	88/–	6	3½	48	Ifauf
36	6	108/–	7¼	4	65	Ifawg

PLAIN SCREW TYPE.

34P	4½	70/6	5	3	35	Ifdal
35P	5¼	85/6	6	3½	48	Ifdia
36P	6	105/6	7¼	4	65	Ifdob

RECORD WORKS - - SHEFFIELD, ENGLAND

C. & J. HAMPTON, LTD.   -   -   MANUFACTURERS

RECORD STEEL VICES

With Steel Swivel Base.

Registered Design No. 666,598.
Swivel Base Patent No. 125,707.

The Swivel Bases of these Vices are made of Steel.

They are of simple construction, and enable the Vice to be swivelled in a complete circle, and can be firmly locked at any point.

QUICK-GRIP TYPE.

Vice No.	Width of Jaws Inches	List Price Each	Opening Inches	Depth of Jaws Inches	Approx. Weight Pounds	Code Word
34S	4½	86/–	5	3	42	Ifbak
35S	5¼	104/–	6	3½	58	Ifbel
36S	6	128/–	7¼	4	72	Ifbra

PLAIN SCREW TYPE.

34PS	4½	84/6	5	3	42	Iflap
35PS	5¼	101/6	6	3½	58	Ifler
36PS	6	125/6	7¼	4	72	Iflis

RECORD WORKS   -   -   SHEFFIELD, ENGLAND

C. & J. HAMPTON, LTD. - - MANUFACTURERS

RECORD STEEL FITTERS' VICE,
No. 84

Stationary Base.   Quick-Grip Type.

Record Steel Vices are specially recommended for Filers and Fitters. They are made of Steel throughout and are unbreakable in use.

The Jaw Plates are secured in position by hexagon-head set-screws, and are renewable and interchangeable.

Width of Jaws $4\frac{1}{2}''$.   Depth of Jaws $3''$.   Opening $5\frac{3}{4}''$.

Approx. Weight 41 pounds.   Code Word : Iffae.

PRICE 75/- each.

RECORD WORKS - - SHEFFIELD, ENGLAND

C. & J. HAMPTON, LTD. - - MANUFACTURERS

RECORD HEAVY-DUTY STEEL VICES

Guaranteed Unbreakable.

These Vices are built to withstand the most arduous conditions, and are eminently suitable for heavy chipping, hammering, etc.

The Body and Sliding Jaw are designed to produce sound and well-braced Steel Castings. The Screw is of large diameter and made of High-Tensile Steel. All working parts are accurately machined and provision is made for lubrication.

QUICK-GRIP TYPE.

Vice No.	Width of Jaws Inches	List Price Each	Opening Inches	Depth of Jaws Inches	Approx. Weight Pounds	Code Word
110	$4\frac{1}{2}$	80/-	5	3	45	Indip
111	$5\frac{1}{4}$	96/-	6	$3\frac{1}{2}$	52	Indor
112	6	115/-	7	$3\frac{3}{4}$	70	Indus
113	7	142/-	8	4	80	Indan
114	8	176/-	9	$4\frac{1}{2}$	95	Indeo

PLAIN SCREW TYPE.

110P	$4\frac{1}{2}$	78/6	5	3	45	Inlaf
111P	$5\frac{1}{4}$	93/6	6	$3\frac{1}{2}$	52	Inleg
112P	6	112/6	7	$3\frac{3}{4}$	70	Inloi
113P	7	139/6	8	4	80	Inluk
114P	8	173/6	9	$4\frac{1}{2}$	95	Inlyl

RECORD WORKS - - SHEFFIELD, ENGLAND

C. & J. HAMPTON, LTD. - - MANUFACTURERS

RECORD HEAVY CHIPPING VICES

This is a powerful Vice of great strength.

It is designed for rough and heavy work in Railroad and Machine Shops, Erecting Shops, Foundries, etc., where heavy duties are imposed upon Vices, such as Pneumatic Chipping, etc.

The Body and Sliding Jaw are Cast Iron.

The Steel Jaw Plates are extra deep, giving large gripping surface, and are "tenoned" on to the Vice (see above illustration), ensuring absolute rigidity.

The Nut is detachable and can be readily renewed.

Vice No.	Width of Jaws Inches	List Price Each	Opening Inches	Depth of Jaws Inches	Approx. Weight Pounds	Code Word
506	6	162/6	10	$4\frac{1}{8}$	120	Ijfen
507	7	230/–	12	$4\frac{3}{4}$	190	Ijflo
$508\frac{1}{2}$	$8\frac{1}{2}$	342/–	12	$5\frac{1}{2}$	265	Ijfop

RECORD WORKS - - SHEFFIELD, ENGLAND

C. & J. HAMPTON, LTD.   -   -   MANUFACTURERS

RECORD STEEL
HEAVY CHIPPING VICES

Guaranteed Unbreakable.

This Steel Vice is a heavy and powerful tool of great strength.

The Body and Sliding Jaw are TOUGH STEEL CASTINGS and the Vice is guaranteed unbreakable.

The Steel Jaw Plates are extra deep, giving large gripping surface, and are "tenoned" on to the Vice (see above illustration), ensuring absolute rigidity.

The Nut is detachable and can be readily renewed.

Vice No.	Width of Jaws Inches	List Price Each	Opening Inches	Depth of Jaws Inches	Approx. Weight Pounds	Code Word
516	6	215/-	10	$4\frac{1}{8}$	120	Ijhao
517	7	295/-	12	$4\frac{3}{4}$	190	Ijhep
$518\frac{1}{2}$	$8\frac{1}{2}$	430/-	12	$5\frac{1}{2}$	265	Ijhir

RECORD WORKS   -   -   SHEFFIELD, ENGLAND

C. & J. HAMPTON, LTD.   -   -   MANUFACTURERS

RECORD COMBINATION VICES

Stationary Base.

This Vice is a combined Bench and Pipe Vice.

The Body, Sliding Jaw and Base Plate are Cast Iron of guaranteed strength.

The Pipe Jaws are machined from tool steel, and are carefully hardened and tested. They can be readily detached to enable the Vice to take deep work between the jaws.

(Continued on next page)

Vice No.	Will grip Pipes Inches	Width of Vice Jaws Inches	List Price Each	Approx. Weight Pounds	Extra Pipe Jaws Set of 3	Code Word
631	$\frac{1}{8}$ to $2\frac{1}{2}$	$3\frac{1}{2}$	63/6	38	10/-	Icrey
632	$\frac{1}{8}$ to $3\frac{1}{2}$	$4\frac{1}{4}$	87/-	68	14/3	Icriz
633	$\frac{1}{8}$ to $4\frac{1}{2}$	5	127/-	112	23/3	Icrom
634	$\frac{1}{8}$ to 6	6	180/-	170	33/3	Icrun

RECORD WORKS   -   -   SHEFFIELD, ENGLAND

C. & J. HAMPTON, LTD. - - MANUFACTURERS

RECORD COMBINATION VICES
With Swivel Base.

The front Pipe Jaw has teeth at both ends and is reversible.

The Parallel Jaw Plates are made of Steel and are extra deep, giving large gripping surface. They are "tenoned" on to the Vice (see above illustration), ensuring absolute rigidity.

The Nut is detachable and can be readily renewed.

The Swivel Base locking arrangement is simple and effective, and the Vice can be locked in any position by means of the wing nut.

Vice No.	Will grip Pipes Inches	Width of Vice Jaws Inches	List Price Each	Approx. Weight Pounds	Extra Pipe Jaws Set of 3	Code Word
631S	$\frac{1}{8}$ to $2\frac{1}{2}$	$3\frac{1}{2}$	66/6	42	10/-	lcvam
632S	$\frac{1}{8}$ to $3\frac{1}{2}$	$4\frac{1}{4}$	92/-	72	14/3	lcven
633S	$\frac{1}{8}$ to $4\frac{1}{2}$	5	133/6	120	23/3	lcvop
634S	$\frac{1}{8}$ to 6	6	187/6	180	33/3	lcvur

RECORD WORKS - - SHEFFIELD, ENGLAND

C. & J. HAMPTON, LTD. - - MANUFACTURERS

RECORD HEAVY-DUTY IRON VICES

Stationary Base.   Plain Screw Type.

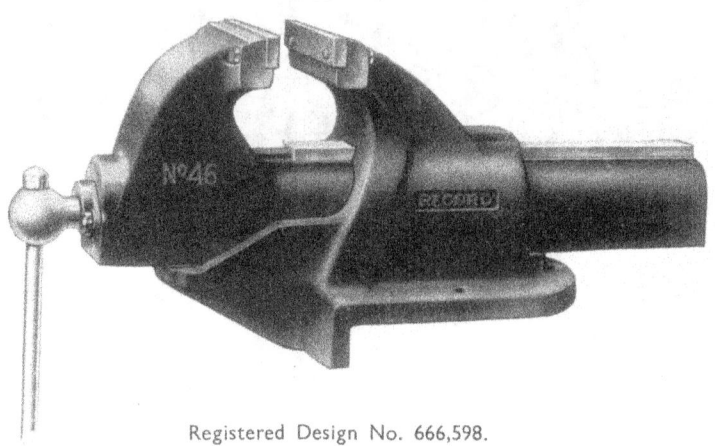

Registered Design No. 666,598.

This Vice is designed expressly for rough and heavy work in foundries and dockyards, and in workshops where heavy duties are imposed upon Vices.

The Nut is detachable and can be readily renewed.

The Jaw Plates of Record Vices are renewable and interchangeable.

Vice No.	Width of Jaws Inches	List Price Each	Opening Inches	Depth of Jaws Inches	Approx. Weight Pounds	Code Word
46	6	120/–	10	4½	125	Igweg
48	8	260/–	12	5½	240	Igwok
49	10	300/–	12	5½	250	Igwaf

RECORD WORKS - - SHEFFIELD, ENGLAND

C. & J. HAMPTON, LTD.   -   -   MANUFACTURERS

RECORD MACHINE VICES

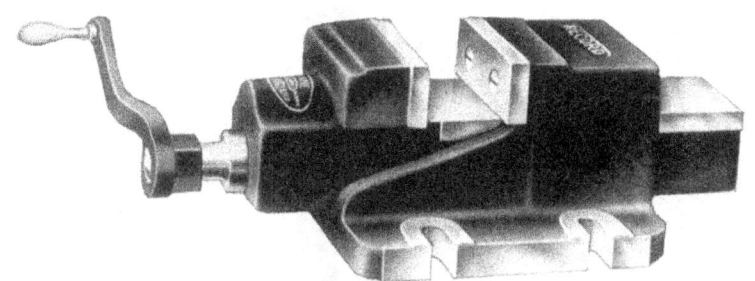

Registered Design No. 725,781.

For use on
Drilling, Milling and Shaping Machines.

This is a compact, sturdy and rigid Machine Vice, and has a perfectly parallel grip. The Front Jaw sliding through the Body prevents the work from lifting when being gripped.

The Screw is entirely enclosed, and the sides of the base are machined at right angles to the jaws to facilitate setting.

Vice No.	Width of Jaws Inches	List Price Each	Depth of Jaws Inches	Opening Inches	Size of Base Inches	Slot Centres of Base Inches	Approx. Weight Pounds	Code Word
*242	2	17/-	$\tfrac{3}{4}$	2	$4 \times 3\tfrac{3}{4}$	$2 \times 3\tfrac{1}{16}$	5	Inbez
*243	3	24/-	$1\tfrac{1}{8}$	$2\tfrac{1}{2}$	$5\tfrac{1}{2} \times 5$	$3 \times 4\tfrac{1}{16}$	13	Inbim
244	4	45/-	$1\tfrac{3}{8}$	$3\tfrac{1}{4}$	$7\tfrac{1}{4} \times 6\tfrac{3}{4}$	$3\tfrac{1}{2} \times 5\tfrac{1}{2}$	28	Inbon
245	5	85/-	$1\tfrac{5}{8}$	4	$8\tfrac{1}{2} \times 8\tfrac{1}{4}$	$4\tfrac{1}{4} \times 6\tfrac{7}{8}$	45	Inbro
246	6	110/-	2	$5\tfrac{1}{8}$	$10\tfrac{1}{4} \times 9\tfrac{1}{2}$	$5\tfrac{1}{4} \times 8$	70	Inbup

* Nos. 242 and 243 are fitted with Drop Handle.

RECORD WORKS   -   -   SHEFFIELD, ENGLAND

C. & J. HAMPTON, LTD. - - MANUFACTURERS

RECORD STAPLE VICES

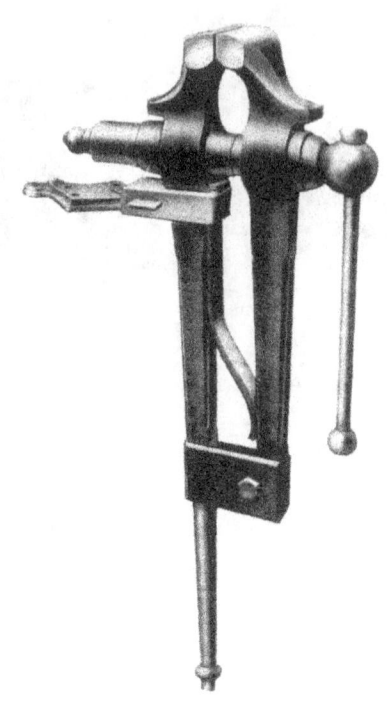

Forged Wrought Iron throughout.

With Solid Box, Solid Steel-faced Jaws, and Steel Screw.

Vice No.	Width of Jaws Inches	List Price Each	Approx. Weight Pounds	Code Word
703	3	56/-	40	Icoar
703½	3½	58/-	40	Icocs
704	4	67/6	56	Icoft
704½	4½	75/-	60	Icoky
705	5	90/-	84	Icolz
706	6	120/-	112	Icorm
707	7	150/-	140	Icown

RECORD WORKS - - SHEFFIELD, ENGLAND

C. & J. HAMPTON, LTD.   -   -   MANUFACTURERS

PORTABLE VICE BENCH
Fig. 550

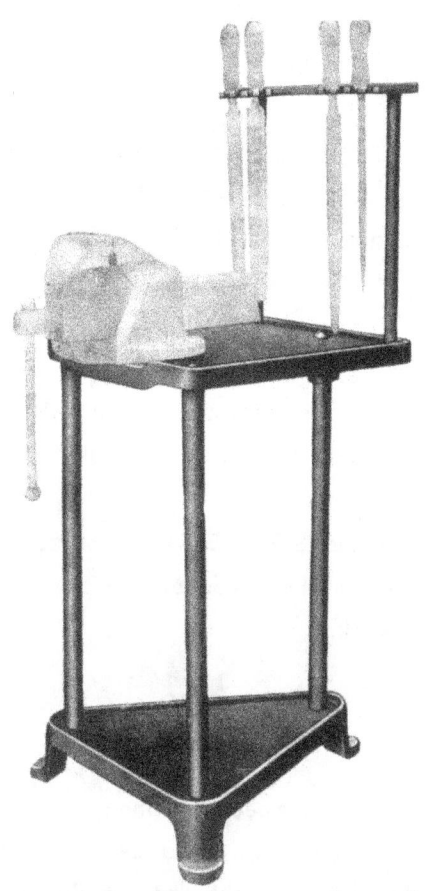

Cast Iron Table and Base.   Wrought Iron Tubular Legs.
Top of Table 18" x 19".   Height of Table 30".

Approximate Weight 110 pounds.   Code Word : Idfog.

PRICE   ...   **70/-** each.

VICE EXTRA according to type and size required.

RECORD WORKS   -   -   SHEFFIELD, ENGLAND

C. & J. HAMPTON, LTD.   -   -   MANUFACTURERS

RECORD STEEL FLOOR VICES

Guaranteed Unbreakable.

The Record Steel Floor Vice is designed to meet the requirements of Railway and Tramway Shops, Locomotive Builders, Wagon Builders, Spring Makers, Constructional Iron Works, Machine Shops, Foundries, Fettling Shops, Forges, Bridge Builders, Collieries, Mines, Rolling Mills, etc.

It is a general utility tool in the general workshop; it stands like an anvil and is accessible for work in any position. Irregularly shaped articles can be held between the jaws, allowing the operator to select the most convenient position for working.

BODY : The body is a one-piece STEEL CASTING, of great strength, well-braced, and is guaranteed unbreakable. The jaw head is built in the form of an arch for the convenience of gripping irregular shaped work.

SLIDING JAW : The sliding jaw is a one-piece STEEL CASTING of great strength.

JAW PLATES : The jaw plates have deep machine-cut serrated faces, and are hardened to obviate the snipping of the jaw edges. The Jaw Plates are secured in position by hexagon-head set-screws; they are renewable and interchangeable. Special plates can be affixed if required.

MAIN SCREW : Made from high-tensile steel.

NUT : Made from material which gives good sliding action with minimum friction; it is detachable and renewable.

RECORD WORKS   -   -   SHEFFIELD, ENGLAND

C. & J. HAMPTON, LTD.   -   -   MANUFACTURERS

RECORD STEEL FLOOR VICES

Guaranteed Unbreakable.

Vice No. 112F.

Width of Jaws 12".   Opening of Jaws 10".

Gap 20" deep x 8" opening.

Approximate Weight 750 pounds.   Code Word : Itwog.

PRICE on application.

RECORD WORKS   -   -   SHEFFIELD, ENGLAND

C. & J. HAMPTON, LTD. - - MANUFACTURERS

FIBRE GRIPS FOR VICES

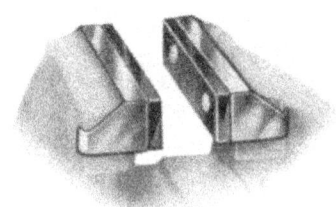

The Steel Lugs bend round the Vice Jaws and secure the Grips in position (as shown in illustration) and will fit any Bench Vice.

These Grips are made of Steel and are fitted with Special Fibre Faces.

This specially prepared Fibre has a cushion face and is far more durable than lead or copper.

Delicate articles or highly polished surfaces can be gripped firmly without fear of damage.

The Fibre Faces are renewable.

Code Word : Islod.

For Vices with width of Jaws	3"	3¼"	3½"	3¾"	4"
PRICE per Pair	2/6	2/6	3/-	3/-	3/-
For Vices with width of Jaws	4¼"	4½"	5"	5¼"	6"
PRICE per Pair	3/6	3/6	4/-	4/-	4/-

Packed 1 pair per box.

RECORD WORKS - - SHEFFIELD, ENGLAND

C. & J. HAMPTON, LTD.   -   -   MANUFACTURERS

STEEL JAW PLATES
For RECORD VICES.

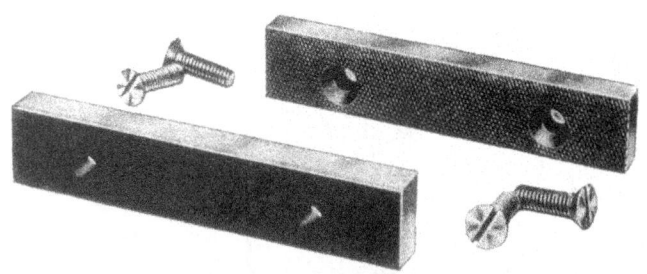

JAW PLATES to suit RECORD VICES.
Code Word : Isleb.

The Steel Jaw Plates of Record Vices are renewable and interchangeable.

When ordering spare Jaw Plates VICE NUMBER must be given ; width of Jaw alone is not sufficient.

To suit Vice No.	Width of Jaws Inches	List Price Per pair	To suit Vice No.	Width of Jaws Inches	List Price Per pair
00	2¼	2/–	46	6	7/–
0	2½	2/–	48	8	14/–
1	3	2/6	49	10	17/6
2	3½	3/–	110	4½	6/–
3	4	3/9	111	5¼	7/–
4	4½	5/–	112	6	8/6
5	5	6/–	242	2	3/6
6	6	7/–	243	3	6/–
7	7	8/6	244	4	8/–
8	8	10/6	245	5	10/–
21	3¼	4/–	246	6	11/6
22	3¾	4/6	506	6	31/–
23	4¼	5/–	507	7	36/–
24	5¼	6/–	508½	8½	46/–
25	6	7/–	516	6	31/–
27	7	8/6	517	7	36/–
28	8	14/–	518½	8½	46/–
34	4½	5/–	631	3½	20/–
35	5¼	6/–	632	4¼	21/–
36	6	7/–	633	5	25/–
			634	6	31/–
34P	4½	5/–	631S	3½	20/–
35P	5¼	6/–	632S	4¼	21/–
36P	6	7/–	633S	5	25/–
			634S	6	31/–

RECORD WORKS   -   -   SHEFFIELD, ENGLAND

C. & J. HAMPTON, LTD. - - MANUFACTURERS

RECORD STEEL BENCH SCREWS
Fig. 165
For WOOD VICES.

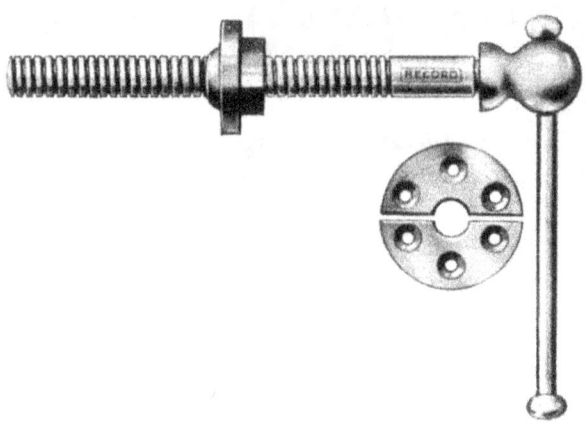

These Bench Screws are of solid Forged Steel, machined all over, and polished bright.

The Nut and Collar are finished black.

Length Overall Inches	Diameter of Screw Inches	List Price Each	Code Word
16	1	10/6	lvlog
18	$1\frac{1}{8}$	14/-	lvrik
20	$1\frac{1}{4}$	17/6	lvrul
22	$1\frac{1}{2}$	29/6	lvsec

RECORD WORKS - - SHEFFIELD, ENGLAND

C. & J. HAMPTON, LTD. - - MANUFACTURERS

RECORD WOODWORKERS' VICES

With Unbreakable Steel Slides.

AN EFFICIENT WOODWORKER'S VICE : The Record Woodworker's Vice meets the demand for a really efficient and dependable Vice for the woodworker's bench.

CONSTRUCTION : The Sliding Bars are SOLID STEEL, machined and polished, and work in accurately machined housings. This gives a perfect sliding movement and a firm and straight grip, eliminating all undesirable side and cross movements. The practicability of this feature is appreciated when operating on accurate work ; for example, pressing into position a glued joint. The Vice has a perfectly parallel grip, and the STEEL SLIDES are placed in such a position under the jaws as to give maximum amount of clearance.

ACTION : It can be used as a quick-acting or screw-all-the-way Vice. Work can be instantly gripped or released at any point by a half-turn of the handle. The Nut which engages with the screw can be instantly released by pressing the trigger, which allows the jaw to slide freely to or from the work. This Vice is also made with Plain Screw Action only.

STRENGTH AND DURABILITY : This Vice is guaranteed to meet the most arduous workshop conditions, and to give long and dependable service.

RECORD WORKS - - SHEFFIELD, ENGLAND

C. & J. HAMPTON, LTD.   -   -   MANUFACTURERS

RECORD WOODWORKERS' VICES

With Unbreakable Steel Slides.

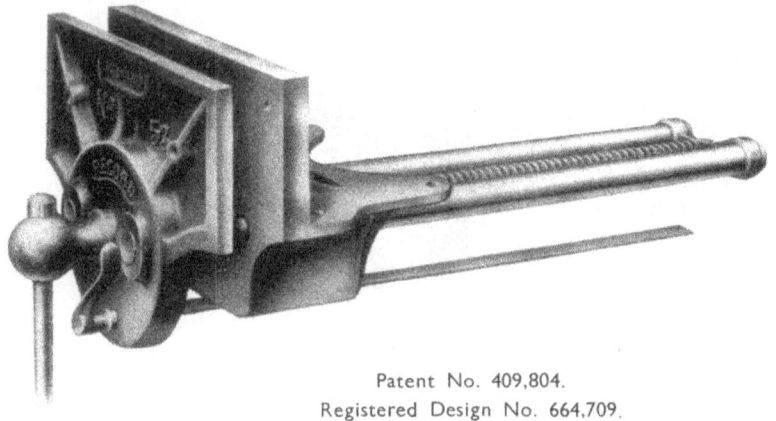

Patent No. 409,804.
Registered Design No. 664,709.

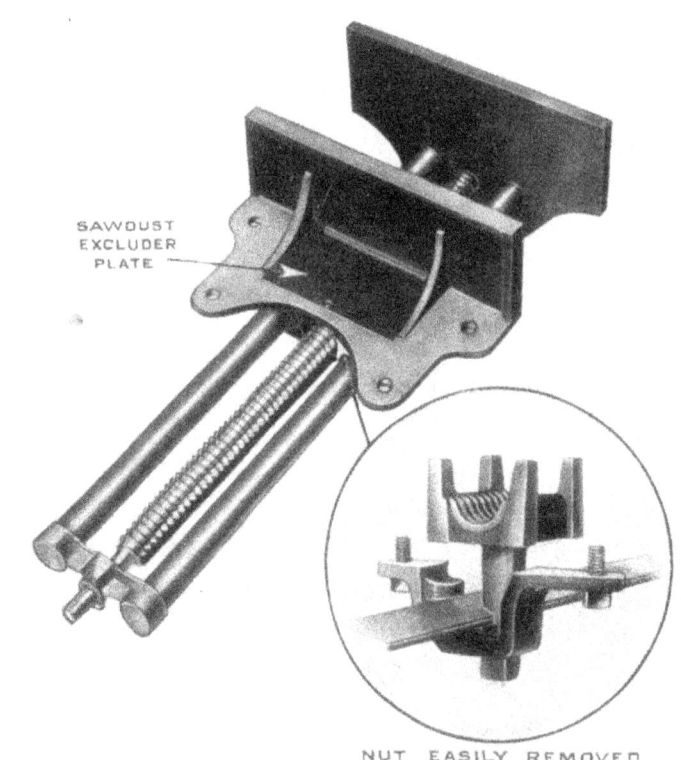

SAWDUST EXCLUDER PLATE

NUT EASILY REMOVED FOR CLEANING

RECORD WORKS   -   -   SHEFFIELD, ENGLAND

C. & J. HAMPTON, LTD. - - MANUFACTURERS

RECORD WOODWORKERS' VICES

With Unbreakable Steel Slides.

Record Woodworkers' Vices are the original and genuine Steel Slide Vices which are now the recognised standard specified by the Woodworking Trades throughout the world.

Behind them is the accumulated experience gained in manufacturing these Vices during many years, and their efficiency and superiority have been tested and proved in service.

The User will appreciate the following NEW FEATURES (see illustration on opposite page) :—

1. A metal plate is fitted into the Body covering the Nut mechanism to prevent sawdust or shavings falling on to the working parts.

2. Improved method of anchoring the Half-Nut which enables it to be quickly taken out for cleaning.

These Vices are made in three types as follows :—

1. With Quick-grip and Continuous Screw Action.

2. With Plain Screw Action only.

3. With Quick-grip and Continuous Screw Action and fitted with Patent Screw and Nut Cover.

QUICK-GRIP TYPE.

Vice No.	Width of Jaws Inches	List Price Each	Opening Inches	Approx. Weight Pounds	Code Word
52	7	22/-	8	18	Iwabs
52½	9	30/-	13	32	Iwadu
53	10½	33/-	15	35	Iweso

RECORD WORKS - - SHEFFIELD, ENGLAND

C. & J. HAMPTON, LTD.   -   -   MANUFACTURERS

RECORD WOODWORKERS' VICES

With Unbreakable Steel Slides.

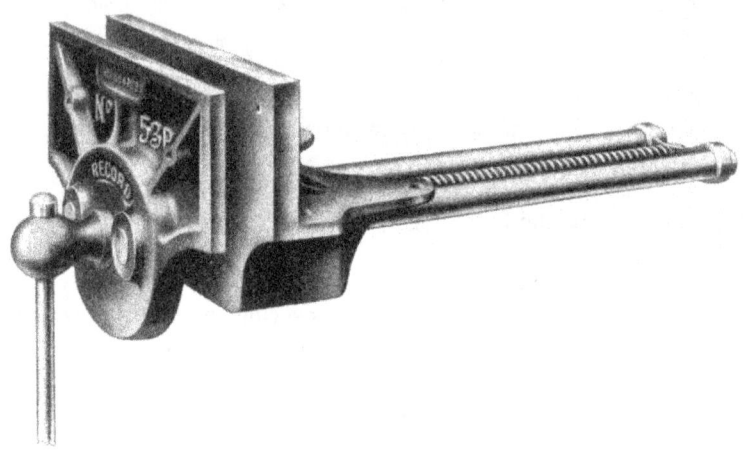

Registered Design No. 664,709.

These Vices are of similar construction to the Quick-Grip type described on pages 105 to 107, but they are fitted with ordinary square thread Screws and Solid Nut, making them screw-all-the-way Vices.

PLAIN SCREW TYPE.

Vice No.	Width of Jaws Inches	List Price Each	Opening Inches	Approx. Weight Pounds	Code Word
52P	7	21/–	8	18	Iwegs
52½P	9	29/–	13	32	Iwelu
53P	10½	32/–	15	35	Iwiky

RECORD WORKS   -   -   SHEFFIELD, ENGLAND

C. & J. HAMPTON, LTD. - - MANUFACTURERS

RECORD WOODWORKERS' VICES

With Patent Screw and Nut Cover.

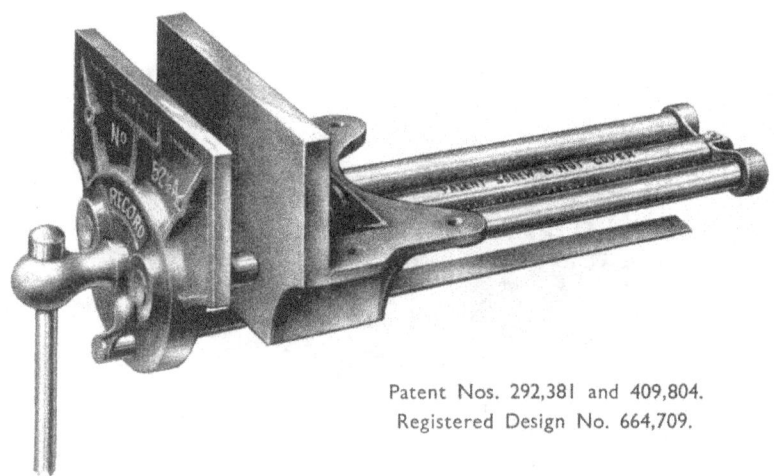

Patent Nos. 292,381 and 409,804.
Registered Design No. 664,709.

These Vices are of similar construction to the Quick-Grip Type described on pages 105 to 107, with the addition of the Patent Screw and Nut Cover.

This Patent Cover extends the entire length of the Screw. It protects both the Screw and Nut from damage, and prevents sawdust and shavings dropping on to the threads and choking these working parts.

WITH PATENT SCREW AND NUT COVER.
(Quick-Grip Vices only).

Vice No.	Width of Jaws Inches	List Price Each	Opening Inches	Approx. Weight Pounds	Code Word
52A	7	24/–	8	18	Iknas
52½A	9	33/–	13	32	Iknet
53A	10½	36/–	15	35	Iknou

RECORD WORKS - - SHEFFIELD, ENGLAND

C. & J. HAMPTON, LTD. - - MANUFACTURERS

RECORD WOODCRAFT VICE
No. 55

This Vice is made on the same lines as the well-known Record Woodworkers' Vices with Unbreakable Steel Slides.

It is fitted with square thread Screw and Solid Nut and is a screw-all-the-way Vice.

Width of Jaws $6\frac{1}{2}''$.   Opening $6\frac{1}{8}''$.   Weight $11\frac{1}{4}$ pounds.

Code Word : Ijeme.

PRICE 11/6 each.

Packed 1 per box.

RECORD WORKS - - SHEFFIELD, ENGLAND

C. & J. HAMPTON, LTD. - - MANUFACTURERS

RECORD AMATEUR WOODWORK VICE, No. 50

Registered Design No. 741,964.

This Vice can be screwed to bench or table.
Slides, Screw and Handle are made of Steel.
Width of Jaws 6".   Opening 4½".   Weight 6½ pounds.
Code Word : Ijeld.

PRICE **7/-** each.

RECORD JUNIOR WOODWORK VICE, No. 51

Patents Nos. 300,392 and 300,494.

This Vice is made with a Clamp so that it can be readily fixed to bench or table.
Slides, Screws and Handle are made of Steel.
Width of Jaws 6".   Opening 4½".   Weight 6 pounds.
Clamp will take from ¾" to 2¼" thick boards.
Code Word : Ijdel.

PRICE **8/6** each.

Packed 1 per box.

RECORD WORKS - - SHEFFIELD, ENGLAND

C. & J. HAMPTON, LTD. - - MANUFACTURERS

RECORD JUNIOR
WOODWORKERS' VICE & CRAMP COMBINED, No. 51c.

1. The RECORD JUNIOR can be fixed to a bench, table, trestle, or post. It will fasten to anything from $\frac{3}{4}''$ to $2\frac{1}{4}''$ thick.
2. It can be carried in a tool kit.
3. The CRAMPING BAR can be readily fixed or detached without removing the Vice from the bench or table.
4. The CRAMP will take work up to 32" in length, and will grip **taper or straight** work as desired.
5. The VICE has a perfectly parallel grip without any side movement.

SPECIFICATION.
Width of Vice Jaws 6".   Opening of Vice Jaws $4\frac{1}{2}''$.
Cramp will take in 32".
Weight 10 pounds.   Code Word : Ijdak.

PRICE COMPLETE ... **14/-**

CRAMPING BAR only (with 2 Jaws) **5/6**

(Note : Cramping Attachment can only be used in conjunction with the Record Junior Vice, as the grip is obtained from the Vice Screw.)

Vice packed in box.

RECORD WORKS - - SHEFFIELD, ENGLAND

C. & J. HAMPTON, LTD. - - MANUFACTURERS

RECORD BENCH STOP,
No. 169

The Record Woodworkers' Bench Stop is easily fixed on the underside of the Bench.

It is supplied complete with Hardwood Block 1½" x 1" which slides through a hole cut in the bench.

The Wing Nut fastens the block in position.

Approx. Weight 2 pounds.   Code Word : lvsid.

PRICE **3/-** each.

RECORD WORKS - - SHEFFIELD, ENGLAND

C. & J. HAMPTON, LTD. - - MANUFACTURERS

REPAIR PARTS for RECORD VICES

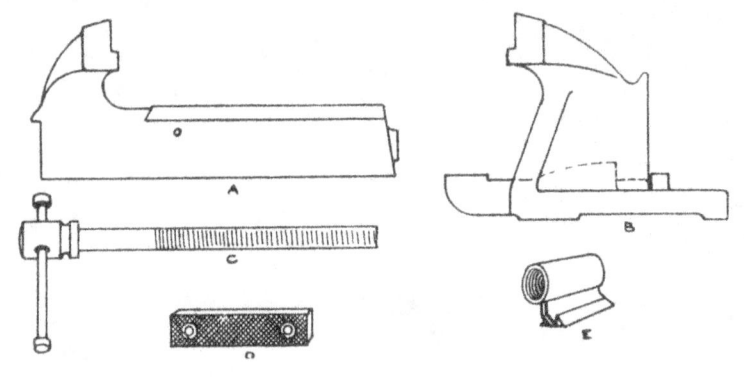

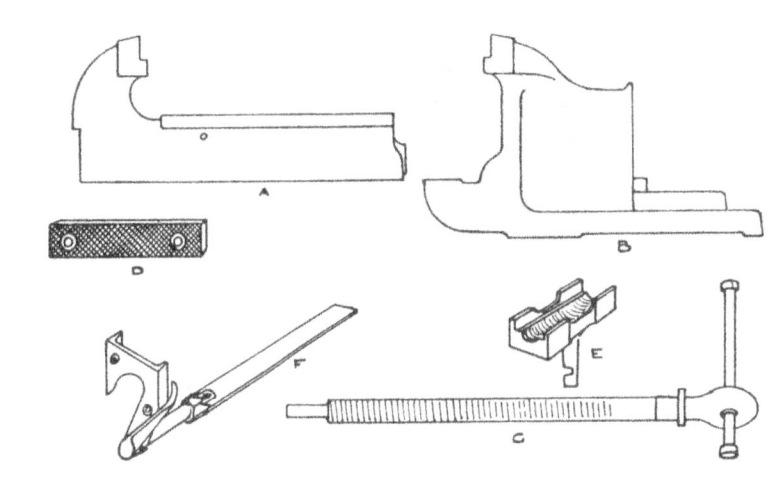

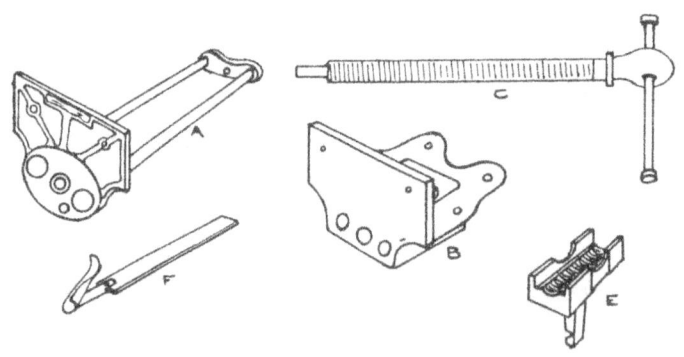

RECORD WORKS - - SHEFFIELD, ENGLAND

C. & J. HAMPTON, LTD. - - MANUFACTURERS

REPAIR PARTS for RECORD VICES

RECORD MECHANICS' VICES (PLAIN SCREW).

	To suit Vice No.									
	00	0	1	2	3	4	5	6	7	8
A. Sliding Jaw	4/6	5/-	6/-	8/6	11/-	14/-	17/6	24/6	29/-	32/-
B. Body	5/6	6/-	7/6	10/6	13/6	17/-	23/6	30/6	36/-	40/-
C. Main Screw and Handle	4/-	4/6	5/-	6/-	7/6	9/-	10/6	12/-	13/6	13/6
D. Jaw Plates (with Set Screws) pair	2/-	2/-	2/6	3/-	3/9	5/-	6/-	7/-	8/6	10/6
E. Nut	1/6	1/9	2/-	2/6	3/-	3/6	4/-	4/6	5/-	5/-
— Spring	6d.	6d.	6d.	6d.	6d.	1/-	1/-	1/-	1/-	1/-

RECORD FITTERS' VICES (QUICK-GRIP).

	To suit Vice No.						
	21	22	23	24	25	27	28
A. Sliding Jaw	13/-	17/-	21/-	25/6	30/6	40/-	60/-
B. Body	14/6	19/-	24/-	30/6	36/-	48/-	72/-
C. Main Screw and Handle	8/6	9/6	11/-	13/-	15/-	18/-	25/-
D. Jaw Plates (with Set Screws) pair	4/-	4/6	5/-	6/-	7/-	8/6	14/-
E. Nut	3/6	4/-	4/6	5/-	5/-	6/-	10/-
F. Trigger, complete with Front Cover Plate, Spring, Adjusting Nut, Rocker Bar and Guide	5/6	6/-	6/6	7/-	7/6	8/-	10/-
— Spring	1/6	1/6	2/-	2/-	2/-	2/-	2/-

RECORD WOODWORKERS' VICES.

	To suit Vice No.		
	52	52½	53
A. Sliding Jaw (complete with Slides)	8/-	12/-	13/-
B. Body	12/-	20/-	21/-
C. Main Screw and Handle	9/-	12/-	12/-
E. Nut	3/6	4/6	4/6
F. Trigger, complete with Spring, Rocker Bar and Guide	3/-	3/6	3/6
— Spring with Adjusting Nut	1/6	2/-	2/-

RECORD WORKS - - SHEFFIELD, ENGLAND

C. & J. HAMPTON, LTD.   -   -   MANUFACTURERS

REPAIR PARTS for RECORD VICES
(Continued).

RECORD STEEL VICE (QUICK-GRIP).

	To suit Vice No.		
	34	35	36
C. Main Screw and Handle	11/-	13/-	15/-
D. Jaw Plates (with Set Screws) ... per pair	5/-	6/-	7/-
E. Nut	4/6	5/-	5/-
F. Trigger, complete with Front Cover Plate, Spring, Adjusting Nut, Rocker Bar and Guide	6/6	7/-	7/6

RECORD STEEL VICE (PLAIN SCREW).

	To suit Vice No.		
	34P	35P	36P
C. Main Screw and Handle	11/-	13/-	15/-
D. Jaw Plates (with Set Screws) ... per pair	5/-	6/-	7/-
E. Nut	4/6	5/-	5/-

RECORD HEAVY-DUTY IRON VICE.

	To suit Vice No.		
	46	48	49
A. Sliding Jaw	50/-	130/-	150/-
B. Body	55/-	140/-	160/-
C. Main Screw and Handle	18/-	30/-	30/-
D. Jaw Plates (with Set Screws) ... per pair	7/-	14/-	17/6
E. Nut	8/-	10/6	10/6
Cover Plate (and Set Screws)	3/-	4/-	4/-

SPARE JAWS to suit RECORD PIPE VICES.

To suit Vice No. 61	2/- each.
,, ,, No. 62	3/- ,,
,, ,, No. 63	5/- ,,
,, ,, No. 64	7/- ,,
,, ,, No. 66	12/- ,,

RECORD WORKS   -   -   SHEFFIELD, ENGLAND

C. & J. HAMPTON, LTD.   -   -   MANUFACTURERS

REPAIR PARTS for RECORD AUTO VICE, No. 74.

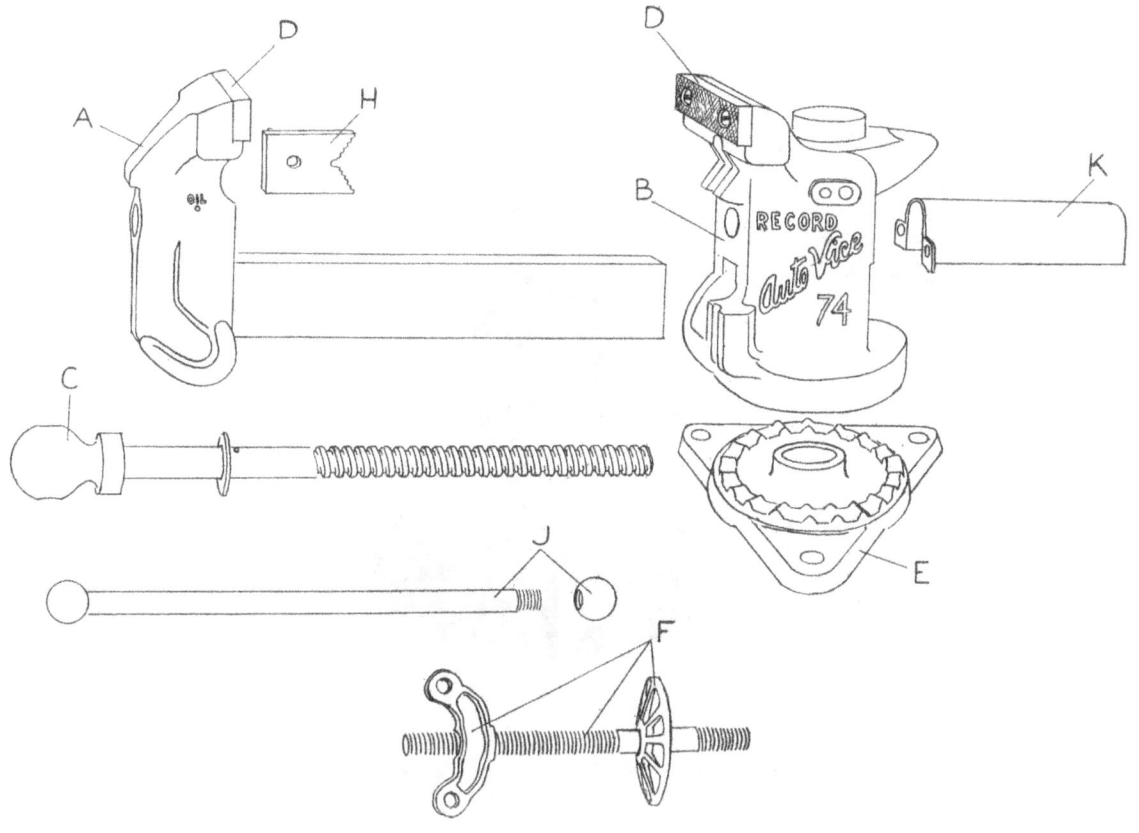

A.	Sliding Jaw, complete with Steel Jaw Plate (D)	10/6
B.	Body, complete with Steel Jaw Plate (D) and Anvil	11/3
C.	Main Screw	6/–
D.	Jaw Plates (per pair)	3/–
E.	Swivel Base Plate	2/3
F.	Screwed Stud, Wing Nut and Washer	2/9
H.	Pipe Grip	1/3
J.	Handle	1/9
K.	Screw Guard	1/3
—	Cylinder Head Holding Plug	2/3

RECORD WORKS   -   -   SHEFFIELD, ENGLAND

C. & J. HAMPTON, LTD.   -   -   MANUFACTURERS

RECORD MOTOR LORRY JACKS

Cast Iron Body and Head of guaranteed strength,
fitted with Steel Screw.

Jack No.	To Lift Tons	Price Each	Range of Lift Inches	Height when down Inches	Diam. of Base Inches	Weight Pounds	Code Word
304	4	17/6	3¾	9	8	20	Ijmer
305	5	19/6	6½	11	8	22	Ijmis

Steel Lever Bars are **1/6** each extra, and only supplied when specified.

RECORD WORKS   -   -   SHEFFIELD, ENGLAND

SECTION 4

PIPE VICES WRENCHES & CUTTERS
Pages 120-134

C. & J. HAMPTON, LTD. - - MANUFACTURERS

RECORD
SELF-LOCKING HINGED PIPE VICES

(Strong Type. Malleable Iron.)

Back View.

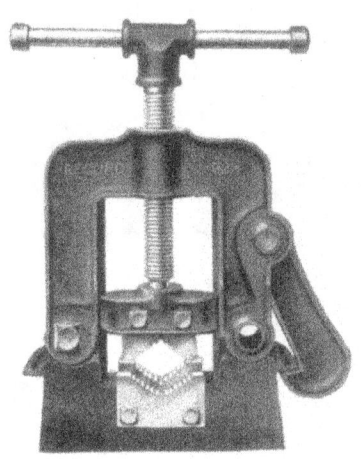

Front View.

These Pipe Vices are designed to withstand the heaviest pipe work, and are guaranteed unbreakable.

They are made of best Malleable Iron, and are fitted with Steel Screw. The Jaws are machined from Tool Steel, and are carefully hardened and tested.

The Frame is reversible so that the Vice can be operated either right or left hand.

The three Jaws are firmly secured into the Base and Head, and ensure an unfailing grip of the pipe.

Three Bolt Holes are provided in the base for fastening to bench or post.

All parts are interchangeable, and are fully guaranteed against defect in material or workmanship.

RECORD WORKS - - SHEFFIELD, ENGLAND

C. & J. HAMPTON, LTD.   -   -   MANUFACTURERS

RECORD
SELF-LOCKING HINGED PIPE VICES

Price List of COMPLETE PIPE VICES.

Vice No.	Will grip Pipes Inches	List Price Each	Approx. Weight Pounds	Extra Jaws (Tool Steel) Set of 3	Code Word
*91	$\frac{1}{8}$ to 1	12/6	4	5/–	Irmek
91$\frac{1}{2}$	$\frac{1}{8}$ to 1$\frac{1}{2}$	15/–	5	6/3	Irlug
92	$\frac{1}{8}$ to 2	17/9	8	7/6	Irmil
92$\frac{1}{2}$	$\frac{1}{8}$ to 2$\frac{1}{2}$	20/9	10	7/6	Irlac
93$\frac{1}{2}$	$\frac{1}{8}$ to 3$\frac{1}{2}$	31/3	18	10/6	Irled
94$\frac{1}{2}$	$\frac{1}{8}$ to 4$\frac{1}{2}$	45/9	25	15/–	Irlie
96	$\frac{1}{8}$ to 6	98/–	40	25/–	Irlof
98	1 to 8	200/–	90	35/6	Irmai
912	1$\frac{1}{2}$ to 12	360/–	200	56/3	Irneb

* No. 91 recommended for Electrical Conduits and Light Service only.

Price List of PARTS.

	To suit Vice No.						
	91	91$\frac{1}{2}$	92	92$\frac{1}{2}$	93$\frac{1}{2}$	94$\frac{1}{2}$	96
Base	5/–	6/–	6/9	8/–	11/9	17/6	37/6
Frame	3/6	3/9	4/2	5/–	7/6	11/–	24/–
Main Screw and Handle	3/–	4/3	5/–	6/–	9/3	12/6	27/6
Locking Hook (with Rivet)	1/–	1/–	1/3	1/6	2/–	3/3	6/9
Jaw Clamps ... pair	2/–	2/–	2/–	2/6	4/–	5/6	10/–
Lower Jaws (Tool Steel) ... each	1/9	2/3	2/6	2/6	3/6	5/–	8/6
Upper Jaws (Tool Steel) ... ,,	1/9	2/3	2/6	2/6	3/6	5/–	8/6

RECORD WORKS   -   -   SHEFFIELD, ENGLAND

C. & J. HAMPTON, LTD. - - MANUFACTURERS

RECORD OPEN-SIDE PIPE VICES

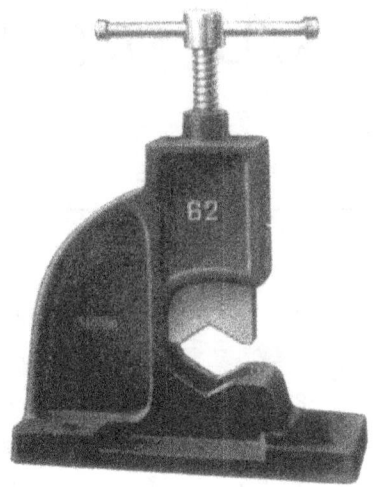

Heavy Type.
Cast Iron.

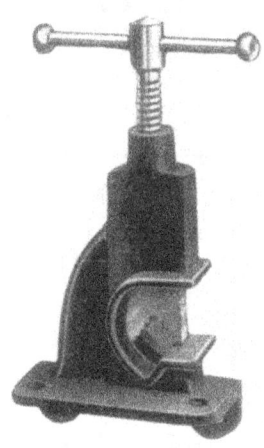

Light Type.
Malleable Iron.

The Jaw is machined from Tool Steel and the Teeth are hardened. The Screw and Handle are made of Steel.

HEAVY TYPE.   Cast Iron.

Vice No.	Will grip Pipes Inches	Approx. Weight Pounds	List Price Each	Code Word
61	$\frac{1}{8}$ to $1\frac{1}{4}$	14	17/6	Ikcyb
62	$\frac{1}{4}$ to 2	30	25/-	Ikdak
63	$\frac{1}{4}$ to 3	45	34/-	Ikded
64	$\frac{1}{4}$ to 4	78	48/-	Ikdie
65	1 to 5	90	62/-	Ikexi
66	1 to 6	130	100/-	Ikfel
68	2 to 8	190	184/-	Ikfla
69	3 to 10	230	240/-	Ikfob

LIGHT TYPE.   Malleable Iron.

31	$\frac{1}{8}$ to 1	5	13/-	Ijkau
31$\frac{1}{2}$	$\frac{1}{8}$ to $1\frac{1}{2}$	10	17/6	Ijkey
32	$\frac{1}{4}$ to 2	13	22/-	Ijkiz

RECORD WORKS - - SHEFFIELD, ENGLAND

C. & J. HAMPTON, LTD. - - MANUFACTURERS

RECORD CHAIN PIPE VICES

Drop-Forged Steel.

These Chain Pipe Vices can be readily fixed to bench or post. They are compact and portable, Nos. 181 and 182 being suitable for carrying in a tool kit.

They are made of Drop-Forged Steel and are unbreakable. The Jaws are carefully hardened and tempered to ensure long life.

The Chains are made of High Tensile Steel and are subjected to special heat treatment. They are tested and guaranteed to give dependable service.

All parts are interchangeable with standard make, and are fully guaranteed against defect in material or workmanship.

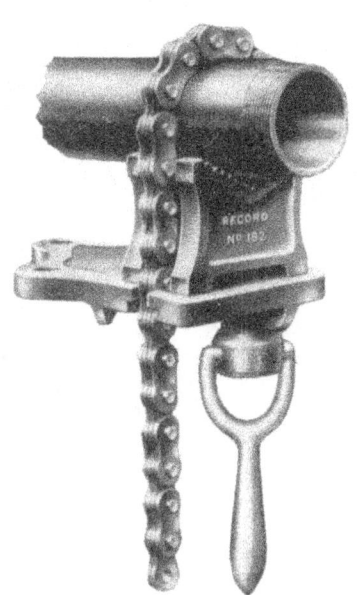

Price List of COMPLETE PIPE VICES.

Vice No.	Capacity Size Pipe Inches	List Price Each	Approx. Weight Pounds	Code Word
181	$\tfrac{1}{8}$ to 2	29/-	4	Ikkab
182	$\tfrac{1}{4}$ to 4	62/6	10	Ikkec
183	$\tfrac{1}{2}$ to 6	112/6	18	Ikkid
184	$\tfrac{1}{2}$ to 8	150/-	30	Ikkoe

Price List of PARTS.

	To suit Chain Pipe Vice No.			
	181	182	183	184
Extra Chain, with Screw	10/6	20/-	37/6	50/-
Extra Jaws ... pair	12/6	29/3	50/-	75/-
Screw	3/6	5/9	10/6	10/6
Handle and Nut	9/3	17/6	29/3	29/3
Nut	5/9	11/3	16/9	16/9

Nos. 181 and 182 packed 1 per Box.

RECORD WORKS - - SHEFFIELD, ENGLAND

C. & J. HAMPTON, LTD. - - MANUFACTURERS

RECORD
FOLDING TRIPOD STANDS

Fitted with Chain Pipe Vices.

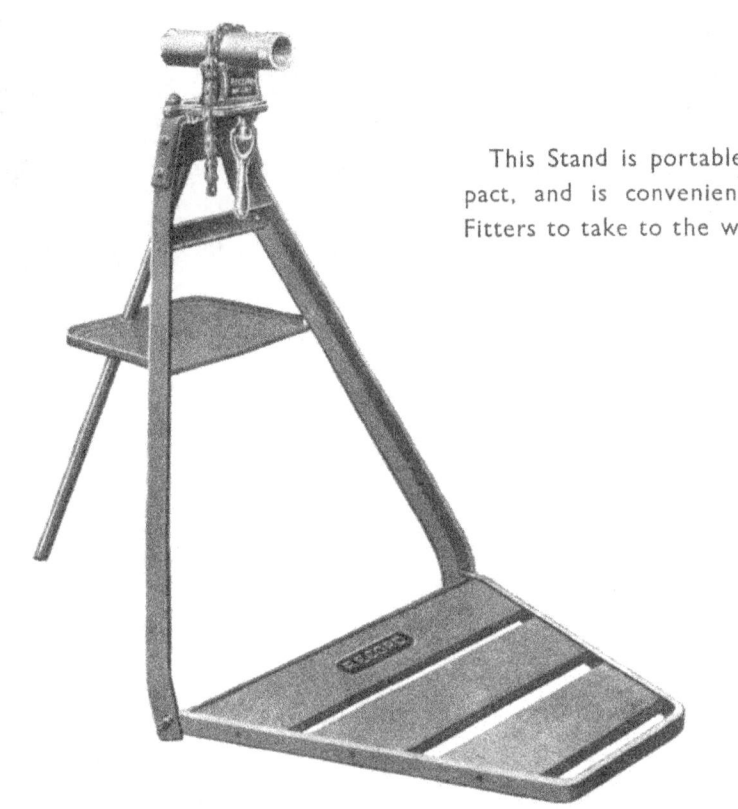

This Stand is portable and compact, and is convenient for Pipe Fitters to take to the work.

	List Price Each Complete	Approx. Weight Pounds	Code Word
No. 581 Stand, fitted with a No. 181 Record Chain Pipe Vice, for $\frac{1}{8}''$ to 2" pipes ...	58/–	40	Idfri
No. 582 Stand, fitted with a No. 182 Record Chain Pipe Vice, for $\frac{1}{4}''$ to 4" pipes ...	95/–	56	Idfif

RECORD WORKS - - SHEFFIELD, ENGLAND

C. & J. HAMPTON, LTD. - - MANUFACTURERS

RECORD
FOLDING TRIPOD STANDS

Fitted with Hinged Pipe Vices.

This Stand is portable and compact, and is convenient for Pipe Fitters to take to the work.

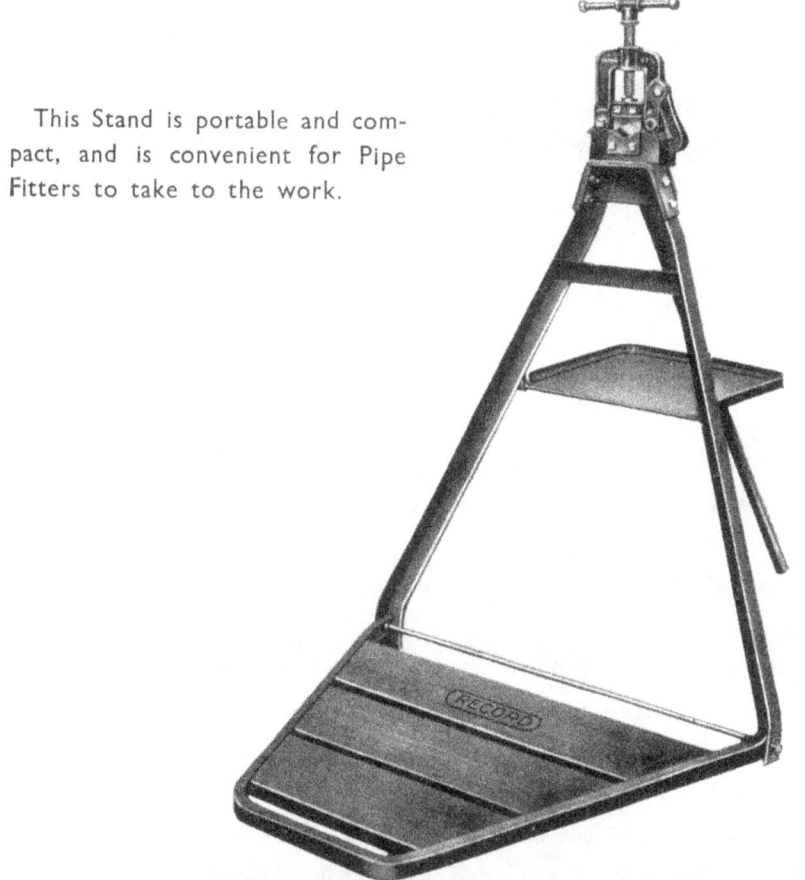

	List Price Each Complete	Approx. Weight Pounds	Code Word
No. 592 Stand, fitted with a No. 92 Record Hinged Pipe Vice, for $\frac{1}{8}''$ to 2″ pipes ...	54/–	45	Ideze
No. 592$\frac{1}{2}$ Stand, fitted with a No. 92$\frac{1}{2}$ Record Hinged Pipe Vice, for $\frac{1}{8}''$ to 2$\frac{1}{2}''$ pipes ...	72/–	56	Idgak

RECORD WORKS - - SHEFFIELD, ENGLAND

C. & J. HAMPTON, LTD.   -   -   MANUFACTURERS

RECORD CHAIN PIPE WRENCHES

With Improved Chain Connection.

(Patent No. 234,392.)

Record Chain Pipe Wrenches are made of Drop-Forged Steel, with Double-Ended Reversible Jaws for gripping pipes, pipe-fittings, etc.

The Jaws are carefully hardened and tempered to ensure long life.

The Chains are made of High Tensile Steel, and are subjected to special heat treatment. They are tested and guaranteed to give dependable service.

The improved Chain Connecting Link swings freely on a sleeve or bush, which is tightened between the prongs of the lever head by the centre stud passing through it. This holds the Jaws absolutely rigid and prevents them from working loose.

All parts are interchangeable with standard make, and are fully guaranteed against defect in material or workmanship.

TESTED AND GUARANTEED.

RECORD WORKS   -   -   SHEFFIELD, ENGLAND

C. & J. HAMPTON, LTD. - - MANUFACTURERS

RECORD CHAIN PIPE WRENCHES

Drop-Forged Steel, Double-Ended Reversible Jaws.

Price List of COMPLETE WRENCHES.

Wrench No.	Capacity Size Pipe Inches	List Price Each	Length Overall Inches	Approx. Weight Pounds	Chain Breaking Strain Pounds	Code Word
230	$\frac{1}{8}$ to $\frac{3}{4}$	21/–	14	$2\frac{3}{8}$	3,500	Ibinc
231	$\frac{1}{8}$ to $1\frac{1}{2}$	29/–	20	$5\frac{3}{4}$	6,800	Ibird
232	$\frac{1}{4}$ to $2\frac{1}{2}$	41/6	27	10	9,600	Ibite
233	$\frac{3}{4}$ to 4	58/6	37	16	12,600	Ibjif
$233\frac{1}{2}$	1 to 6	75/–	$44\frac{1}{2}$	24	14,100	Ibjog
234	$1\frac{1}{2}$ to 8	91/6	$50\frac{1}{2}$	32	15,800	Ibkei
235	2 to 12	150/–	$64\frac{1}{2}$	50	21,600	Ibkik
*216	4 to 18	333/6	87	140	40,000	Ibkol

* No. 216 Wrench supplied with Non-Reversible Jaws.

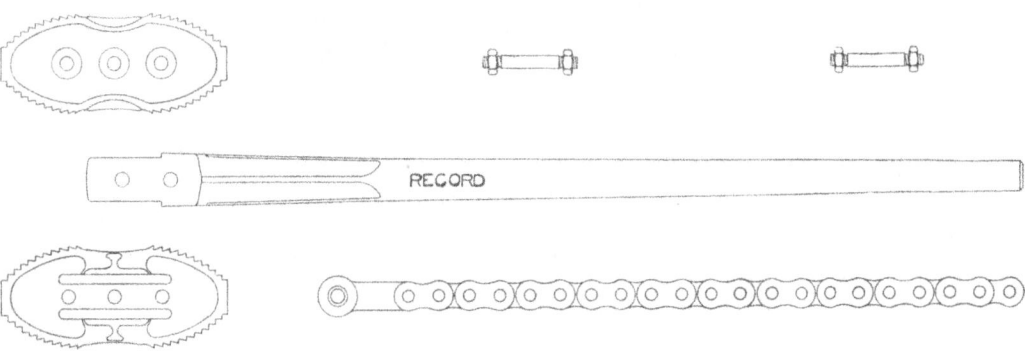

Price List of PARTS.

		To suit Wrench No.							
		230	231	232	233	$233\frac{1}{2}$	234	235	216
Extra Chains	each	6/3	8/3	12/6	21/–	29/–	37/6	62/6	166/6
Extra Jaws	pair	8/3	14/6	23/–	33/3	39/6	45/9	62/6	133/6
Extra Studs and Nuts	set	1/9	2/–	3/–	3/9	4/6	5/9	7/6	10/6
Extra Handles	each	7/–	10/–	13/–	18/–	24/–	30/–	53/–	130/–

RECORD WORKS - - SHEFFIELD, ENGLAND

C. & J. HAMPTON, LTD. - - MANUFACTURERS

RECORD STILLSON PIPE WRENCHES

DROP-FORGED STEEL.

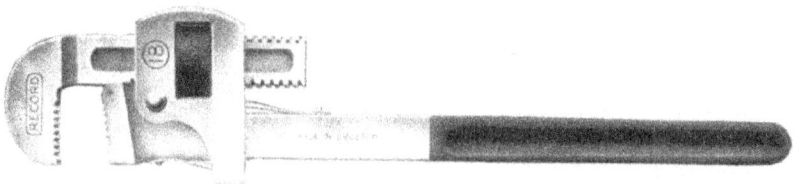

Fig. 300. With Steel Handle.
Made in sizes, 8, 10, 14, 18, 24, 36, 48 inches.

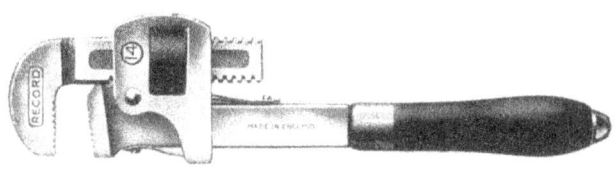

Fig. 400. With Wood Handle.
Made in sizes, 6, 8, 10, 14 inches.

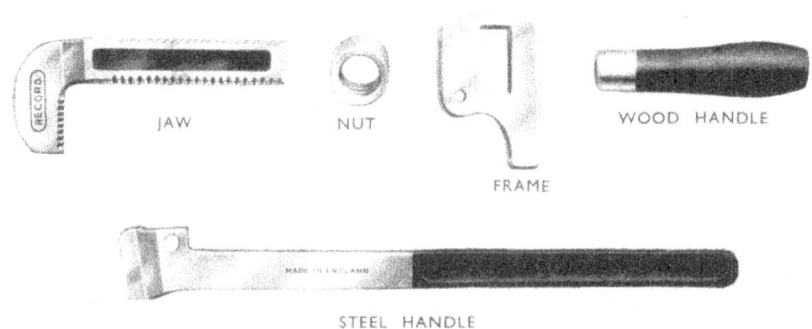

RECORD WORKS - - SHEFFIELD, ENGLAND

C. & J. HAMPTON, LTD. - - MANUFACTURERS

RECORD STILLSON PIPE WRENCHES

DROP-FORGED STEEL.

These Wrenches are made in two styles, Steel Handle and Wood Handle.

Wrenches 8″ and above supplied with Steel Handles unless otherwise specified.

The success of Record Stillson Wrenches is largely due to the high-class quality of Sheffield Steel put into them and to the scientific heat treatment of all the parts.

The Handle and Jaw are subjected to various processes of heat treatment, which imparts the correct degree of hardness to the gripping teeth, and gives to the parts that toughness which prevents breaking, and makes them difficult to bend.

These Wrenches are guaranteed against defect in material and workmanship, and all parts are interchangeable with other standard makes.

STEEL HANDLE WRENCH Fig. 300.

Length when Open Inches	Will grip Pipes Inches	List Price Each	Code Word
8	1/8 to 3/4	9/3	Idjue
10	1/8 to 1	12/-	Idkaf
14	1/4 to 1 1/2	16/-	Idkeg
18	1/4 to 2	23/-	Idkli
24	1/4 to 2 1/2	39/6	Idkok
36	1/4 to 3 1/2	83/6	Idkul
48	1 to 5	125/-	Idkya

WOOD HANDLE WRENCH Fig. 400.

Length when Open Inches	Will grip Pipes Inches	List Price Each	Code Word
6	1/8 to 1/2	8/4	Idvar
8	1/8 to 3/4	9/6	Idves
10	1/8 to 1	13/3	Idvit
14	1/4 to 1 1/2	17/9	Idvou

Wrenches 6″ to 18″ packed 1 per box.

Price List of PARTS.

		To suit Pipe Wrench.							
		6″	8″	10″	14″	18″	24″	36″	48″
Jaws	each	2/9	2/11	4/7	6/3	9/-	14/7	23/9	37/6
Frame and Pin	,,	1/11	2/4	2/11	3/4	4/-	7/4	11/6	14/7
Wood Handles	,,	1/-	1/1	1/3	1/6	—	—	—	—
Steel Handles, with Spring	,,	—	4/10	6/8	9/2	13/7	21/6	43/9	70/10
Nuts	,,	8d.	8d.	10d.	1/3	1/6	2/4	4/7	8/4
Springs	set	3d.	3d.	9d.	9d.	1/-	1/-	9d.	1/-

RECORD WORKS - - SHEFFIELD, ENGLAND

C. & J. HAMPTON, LTD. - - MANUFACTURERS

RECORD
THREE-WHEEL PIPE CUTTERS

With Fast Cutting Wheels.

Record Three-Wheel Pipe Cutters are suitable for work where the tool cannot be revolved all round the pipe.

The special feature is the RECORD FAST CUTTING WHEEL. The design of this Wheel has been developed by extensive experiments and the reduction in the thickness of the cutting edge speeds up cutting, and is only made possible by the use of a better Steel, which is specially Heat-treated.

This method produces a Wheel which cuts faster and lasts longer.

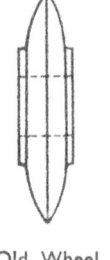

Old Wheel.

Record
Fast-Cutting Wheel.

These Pipe Cutters are individually tested for cutting in line, and are guaranteed against defect in material or workmanship.

All Record Wheels and Pins, and other parts of these Pipe Cutters, are interchangeable with the standard American make.

RECORD WORKS - - SHEFFIELD, ENGLAND

C. & J. HAMPTON, LTD.   -   -   MANUFACTURERS

RECORD
THREE-WHEEL PIPE CUTTERS

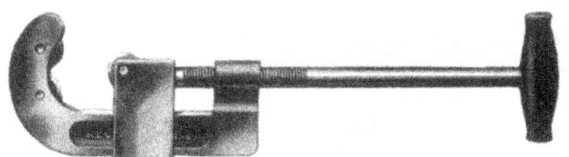

Nos. 101 and 102.

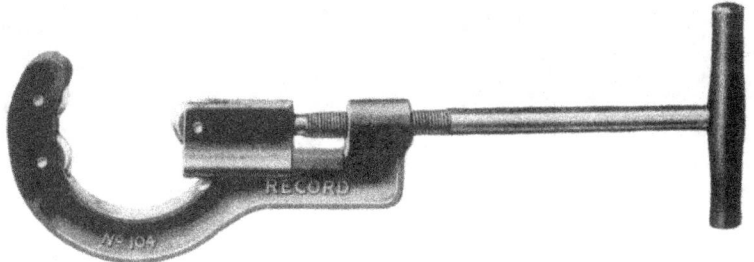

Nos. 103, 104, 105 and 106.

Price List of COMPLETE PIPE CUTTERS.

Cutter No.	Will cut Pipes Inches	List Price Each	Approx. Weight Pounds	Code Word
101	$\frac{1}{8}$ to 1	18/9	3	Insal
102	$\frac{1}{2}$ to 2	25/-	$4\frac{1}{2}$	Insib
103	$1\frac{1}{2}$ to 3	42/-	$8\frac{1}{2}$	Insoc
104	$2\frac{1}{2}$ to 4	84/-	14	Insud
105	4 to 6	125/-	23	Inswe
106	6 to 8	166/-	28	Insyf

Nos. 101 and 102 packed 1 per box.

Price List of PARTS.

		To suit Pipe Cutter No.					
		101	102	103	104	105	106
Wheels	doz.	12/6	15/-	20/-	25/-	37/6	37/6
Wheel Pins	,,	4/3	4/3	4/3	8/3	8/3	8/3
Hook (without Wheels or Pins)	each	7/3	10/9	19/-	39/6	57/3	83/6
Slide and Wheel	,,	3/3	4/3	8/3	18/9	29/3	35/6
Handle and Screw	,,	4/3	5/3	9/6	18/9	29/3	38/6

RECORD WORKS   -   -   SHEFFIELD, ENGLAND

C. & J. HAMPTON, LTD. - - MANUFACTURERS

RECORD LINK PIPE CUTTERS

Fig. 45. As fixed on 4" Pipe.

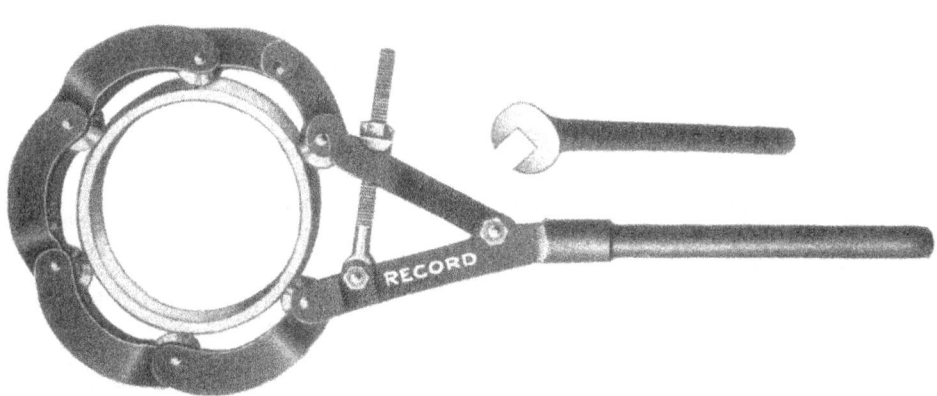

Fig. 46. As fixed on 7" Pipe.

These Pipe Cutters are individually tested for cutting in line and are guaranteed against defect in material or workmanship.

All parts are interchangeable with other standard makes.

RECORD WORKS - - SHEFFIELD, ENGLAND

C. & J. HAMPTON, LTD. - - MANUFACTURERS

RECORD LINK PIPE CUTTERS

	Will cut Pipes Inches	No. of Wheels	List Price Each	Code Word
Fig. 045	½ to 1	3	27/6	Idply
	½ to 1½	4	31/6	Idpoz
	½ to 2	5	35/6	Idpum
Fig. 45	2 to 3	5	40/–	Idnam
	2 to 4	6	45/–	Idnen
	2 to 5	7	50/–	Idnio
	2 to 6	8	55/–	Idnop
	2 to 7	9	60/–	Idnur
	2 to 8	10	65/–	Idnys
Fig. 45A	Three Short Links and Three Wheels to increase the cutting range of Fig. 45 down to ½-in.		12/6	Idomo
Figs. 45 & 45A combined	½ to 3	8	52/6	Igmar
	½ to 4	9	57/6	Igmes
	½ to 5	10	62/6	Igmit
	½ to 6	11	67/6	Igmou
	½ to 7	12	72/6	Igmuy
	½ to 8	13	77/6	Ignaz
Fig. 46	5 to 6	5	65/–	Igulc
	5 to 7	6	72/6	Igumd
	5 to 8	7	80/–	Igupe
	5 to 10	8	87/6	Igurf
	5 to 11	9	95/–	Igusg
	5 to 13	10	102/6	Iguti
Fig. 47 (Extra large size with two handles)	12 to 14	9	157/6	Igpep
	12 to 16	10	170/–	Igpir
	12 to 18	11	182/6	Igpos
	12 to 20	12	195/–	Igput
	12 to 22	13	207/6	Igsiz
	12 to 24	14	220/–	Igsum

Price List of PARTS.

		To suit Pipe Cutter Fig.			
		045	45	46	47
Wheels	each	1/6	1/6	2/3	3/–
Pins	,,	6d.	6d.	7d.	7d.
Shouldered Links	,,	4/6	5/3	8/–	12/–
End Links	,,	5/–	6/–	9/–	10/6
Handle complete	,,	10/–	10/–	19/6	32/6
,, (Lever portion)	,,	—	—	7/6	7/6
,, (Socket portion)	,,	—	—	12/–	25/–
Claw	,,	4/6	4/6	8/6	14/–
Spanner (for large Pipe Cutters only)	,,	—	—	1/6	1/6

RECORD WORKS - - SHEFFIELD, ENGLAND

C. & J. HAMPTON, LTD. - - MANUFACTURERS

DISPLAY STAND for
RECORD STILLSON PIPE WRENCHES

This Display Stand is supplied free with an order for assorted Stillson Wrenches.

RECORD WORKS - - SHEFFIELD, ENGLAND

SECTION 5

BOLT CLIPPERS
Pages 136-142

C. & J. HAMPTON, LTD. - - MANUFACTURERS

RECORD BOLT CLIPPERS,
NUT SPLITTERS and CHAIN CUTTERS

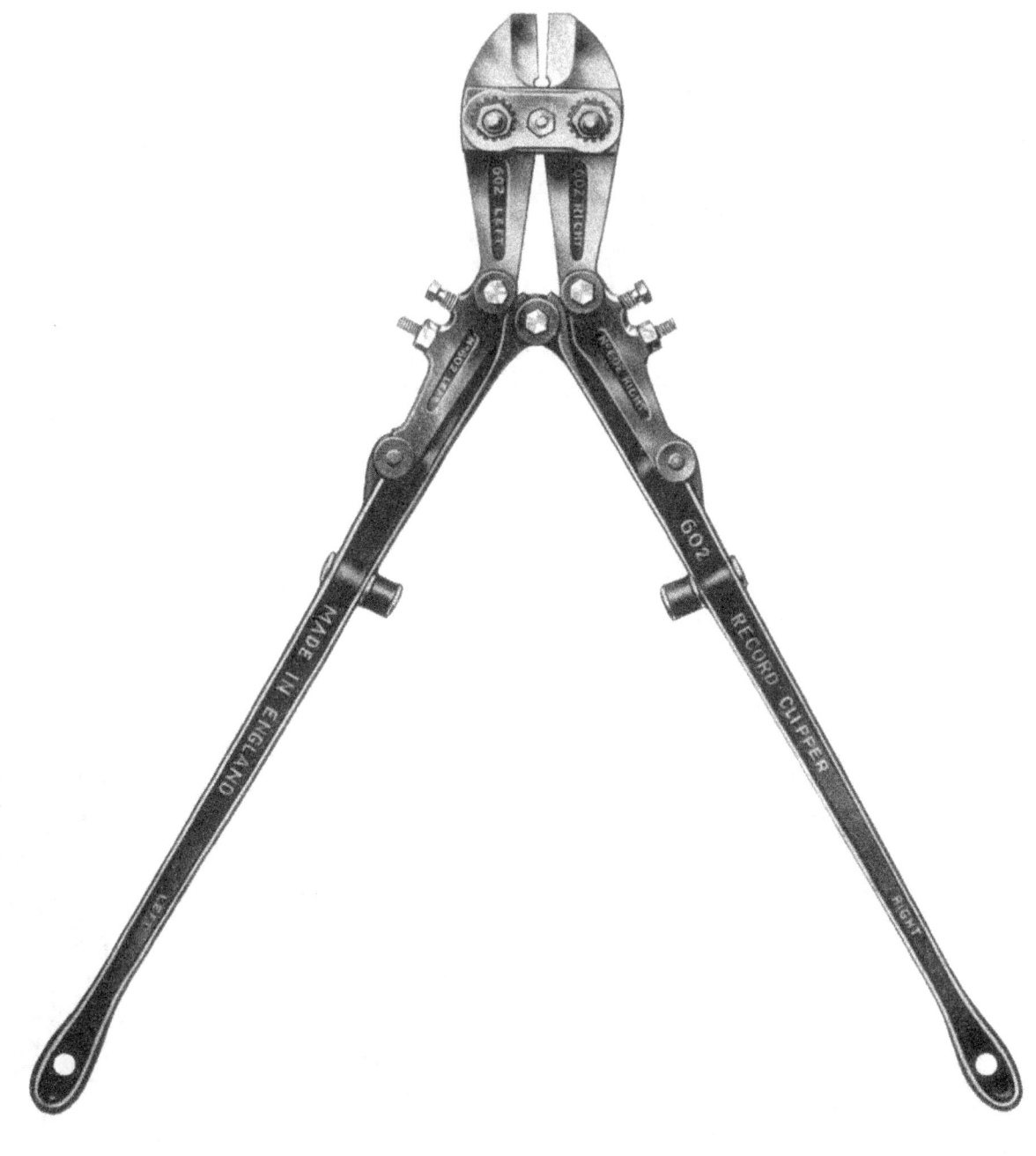

RECORD WORKS - - SHEFFIELD, ENGLAND

C. & J. HAMPTON, LTD.   -   -   MANUFACTURERS

RECORD BOLT CLIPPERS, NUT SPLITTERS and CHAIN CUTTERS

DESIGN AND INTERCHANGEABILITY.

Record Bolt Clippers are of standard American design and all parts are interchangeable.

Record Bolt Clippers are of high grade quality and finish and are guaranteed against defect in material or workmanship.

JAWS.

The Jaws are made of special Tool Steel, scientifically heat-treated, and precision ground on each side and on the cutting edge, and each Jaw is tested to ensure correct temper, toughness and for proper cutting.

The Top and Bottom Straps are hardened steel and are precision ground all over to give perfect fitting and smooth working.

CLIPPER CUT JAWS.

This is the standard type of Jaw and is suitable for general purposes. It is always supplied unless another type of Jaw is specified.

Clipper Cut Jaws are designed for close cutting, having a short bevel on the one side and a long bevel on the opposite side.

When other than soft materials are to be cut, such as spring wire, etc., Jaws of a special temper are required and should be clearly specified when ordering.

CENTRE CUT JAWS.

These Jaws are bevelled equally on each side, bringing the Cutting Edge in the middle. This form of Cutting Edge gives additional strength for heavy work and when cutting hard materials.

NUT SPLITTER JAWS.

These are for splitting square and hexagon nuts to remove them from bolts. When in operation the tool is in line with the bolt.

CHAIN CUTTER JAWS.

These Jaws are made in two types, viz., to cut soft chain, and to cut hard chain. The Jaws for soft chain are not suitable for cutting hard chain, and requirements should be clearly stated when ordering.

RECORD WORKS   -   -   SHEFFIELD, ENGLAND

C. & J. HAMPTON, LTD. - - MANUFACTURERS

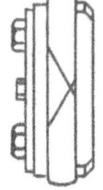

No.		Price complete Each	To cut Bolts on Threads Ins.diam.	To cut Soft Steel Rods Ins.diam.	Length Overall Inches	Approx. Weight Pounds	Code Word
600	Bolt Clippers, with Clipper Cut Jaws ...	23/-	5/16	1/4	18	3¼	Igyfa
601	,, ,, ,, ,, ...	29/3	3/8	5/16	24	5¼	Igylb
602	,, ,, ,, ,, ...	36/6	1/2	3/8	30	8½	Igync
603	,, ,, ,, ,, ...	46/9	5/8	1/2	36	12½	Igyrd

IMPORTANT.—Bolt Clippers with Clipper Cut Jaws are always supplied unless otherwise ordered.

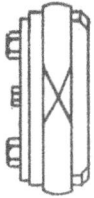

600-CC	Bolt Clippers, with Centre Cut Jaws.	24/-	5/16	1/4	18	3¼	Igval
601-CC	,, ,, ,, ,, ...	30/3	3/8	5/16	24	5¼	Igvib
602-CC	,, ,, ,, ,, ...	37/6	1/2	3/8	30	8½	Igvoc
603-CC	,, ,, ,, ,, ...	49/-	5/8	1/2	36	12½	Igvud

			To split Nuts Sizes				
600-SNS	Side Nut Splitter	26/-	5/16		18	3¼	Iklek
601-SNS	,, ,, ...	32/3	3/8		24	5¼	Iklil
602-SNS	,, ,, ...	39/6	1/2		30	8½	Iklom
603-SNS	,, ,, ...	52/-	5/8		36	12½	Iklun

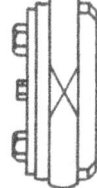

			To cut Chain Links Ins.diam.				
600-SCC	Soft Chain Cutter	25/-	1/4		18	3¼	Imbin
601-SCC	,, ,, ...	31/3	5/16		24	5¼	Imblo
602-SCC	,, ,, ...	38/6	3/8		30	8½	Imbop
603-SCC	,, ,, ...	51/-	1/2		36	12½	Imbur

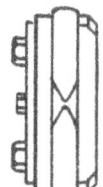

			To cut Chain Links Ins.diam.				
600-HCC	Hard Chain Cutter	25/-	1/4		18	3¼	Inwep
601-HCC	,, ,, ...	31/3	5/16		24	5¼	Inwir
602-HCC	,, ,, ...	38/6	11/32		30	8½	Inwos
603-HCC	,, ,, ...	51/-	7/16		36	12½	Inwut

Numbers 600 to 602 packed 1 per box.   Spare Parts on page 141.

RECORD WORKS - - SHEFFIELD, ENGLAND

C. & J. HAMPTON, LTD. - - MANUFACTURERS

RECORD BOLT CLIPPERS, NUT SPLITTERS and CHAIN CUTTERS

No.		Price complete Each	To cut Bolts on Threads Ins. diam.	To cut Soft Steel Rods Ins. diam.	Length Overall Inches	Approx. Weight Pounds	Code Word
604	Bolt Clippers, with Clipper Cut Jaws	64/6	3/4	5/8	42	19	Imreg
604-CC	,, ,, with Centre Cut Jaws	68/9	3/4	5/8	42	19	Imtut

			To split Nuts Sizes			
604-SNS Side Nut Splitter	... ...	73/-	3/4	42	19	Imzes

			To cut Chain Links Ins. diam.			
604-SCC Soft Chain Cutter	... ...	71/9	5/8	42	19	Inpil

			To cut Chain Links Ins. diam.			
604-HCC Hard Chain Cutter ...	... ...	71/9	1/2	42	19	Inzis

Spare Parts on page 142.

RECORD WORKS - - SHEFFIELD, ENGLAND

C. & J. HAMPTON, LTD. - - MANUFACTURERS

RECORD BOLT CLIPPERS, NUT SPLITTERS and CHAIN CUTTERS

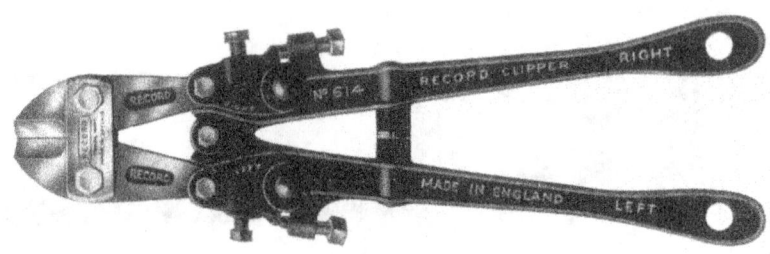

No.		Price complete Each	To cut Bolts on Threads Ins.diam.	To cut Soft Steel Rods Ins.diam.	Length Overall Inches	Approx. Weight Pounds	Code Word
610	Bolt Clippers, with Clipper Cut Jaws ...	16/9	$\frac{3}{16}$	$\frac{1}{8}$	10	$1\frac{3}{4}$	Impud
614	,, ,, ,, ,, ...	18/9	$\frac{1}{4}$	$\frac{3}{16}$	14	$2\frac{1}{2}$	Imraf

IMPORTANT.—Bolt Clippers with Clipper Cut Jaws are always supplied unless otherwise ordered.

| 610-CC | Bolt Clippers, with Centre Cut Jaws. | 17/9 | $\frac{3}{16}$ | $\frac{1}{8}$ | 10 | $1\frac{3}{4}$ | Imtep |
| 614-CC | ,, ,, ,, ,, ... | 19/9 | $\frac{1}{4}$ | $\frac{3}{16}$ | 14 | $2\frac{1}{2}$ | Imtos |

			To split Nuts Sizes				
614-SNS	Side Nut Splitter	21/9	$\frac{1}{4}$		14	$2\frac{1}{2}$	Imzar

			To cut Chain Links Ins.diam.				
610-SCC	Soft Chain Cutter	18/9	$\frac{1}{8}$		10	$1\frac{3}{4}$	Inpai
614-SCC	,, ,, ...	20/9	$\frac{3}{16}$		14	$2\frac{1}{2}$	Inpek

			To cut Chain Links Ins.diam.				
610-HCC	Hard Chain Cutter	18/9	$\frac{1}{8}$		10	$1\frac{3}{4}$	Inzap
614-HCC	,, ,, ...	20/9	$\frac{3}{16}$		14	$2\frac{1}{2}$	Inzer

Packed 1 per box.   Spare Parts on page 142.

RECORD WORKS - - SHEFFIELD, ENGLAND

C. & J. HAMPTON, LTD. - - MANUFACTURERS

PARTS for
RECORD BOLT CLIPPERS, Etc.
Nos. 600 to 603.

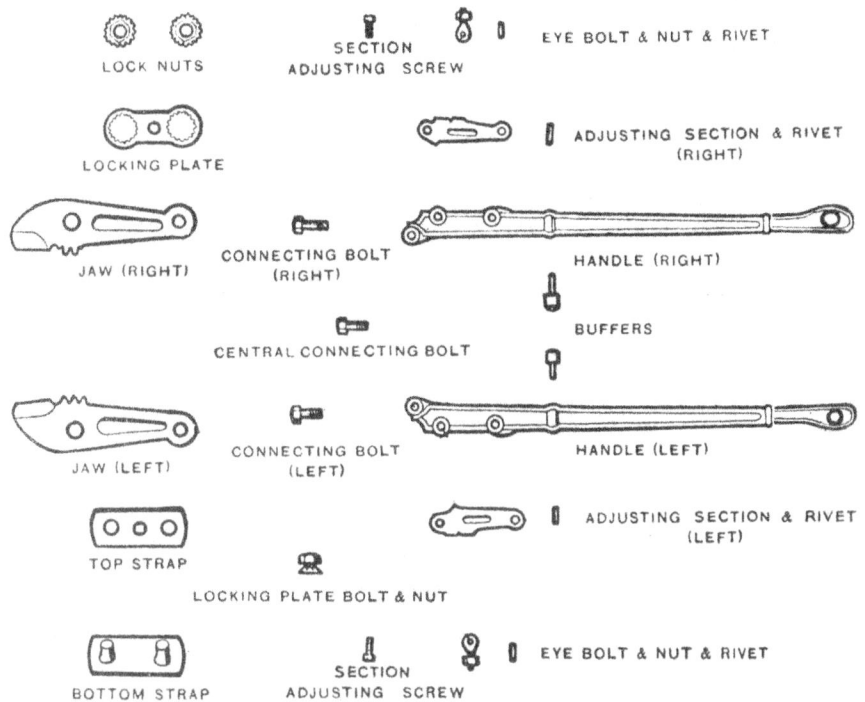

SPARE PARTS PRICE LIST.

To suit No.		600	601	602	603
Jaws, Bolt Clipper, Clipper Cut, Right and Left	pair	10/6	13/3	16/9	20/9
Jaws, Bolt Clipper, Centre Cut, Right and Left	,,	11/3	14/6	18/3	22/9
Jaws, Side Nut Splitter, Right and Left	,,	13/3	17/–	21/3	26/3
Jaws, Soft Chain, Right and Left	,,	12/6	16/3	20/6	25/6
Jaws, Hard Chain, Right and Left	,,	12/6	16/3	20/6	25/6
Bottom Strap with Bolts and Lock Nuts	each	4/2	4/9	5/4	6/–
Top Strap	,,	2/3	2/6	2/9	3/–
Locking Plate	,,	8d.	8d.	9d.	10d.
Locking Plate Bolt and Nut	,,	4d.	4d.	4d.	4d.
Lock Nuts	pair	1/–	1/3	1/6	1/9
Handles (Pair complete with Fittings)	,,	15/6	18/9	23/–	29/3
Handle, Right, without Fittings	each	4/2	5/8	6/10	9/7
Handle, Left, without Fittings	,,	4/2	5/8	6/10	9/7
Adjusting Section (Right) and Rivet	,,	2/3	2/6	2/11	3/4
Adjusting Section (Left) and Rivet	,,	2/3	2/6	2/11	3/4
Centre Connecting Bolt (Right Thread)	,,	8d.	9d.	10d.	1/5
Connecting Bolt (Right Side, Left Thread)	,,	8d.	9d.	10d.	1/5
Connecting Bolt (Left Side, Right Thread)	,,	8d.	9d.	10d.	1/5
Eye Bolt, Nut and Rivet	pair	2/–	2/3	2/5	2/8
Buffers, Washers and Rivets	,,	1/5	1/6	1/7	1/8
Section Adjusting Screw	each	8d.	9d.	10d.	1/5

All Spares are interchangeable with American make.

RECORD WORKS - - SHEFFIELD, ENGLAND

C. & J. HAMPTON, LTD. - - MANUFACTURERS

PARTS for RECORD BOLT CLIPPERS, Etc.
Nos. 604, 610 and 614.

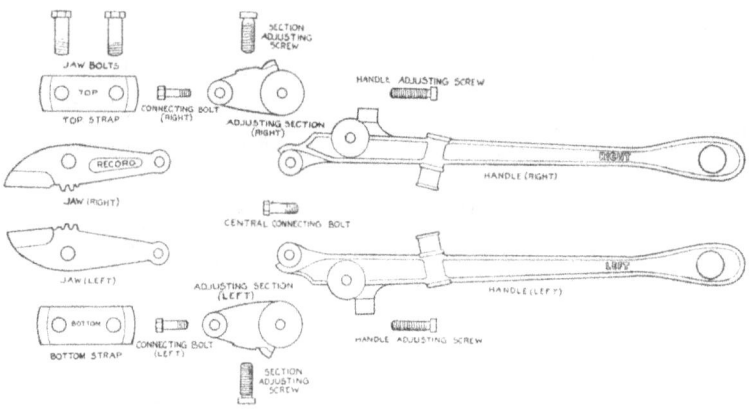

SPARE PARTS PRICE LIST.

To suit No.	604	610	614
Jaws, Bolt Clipper, Clipper Cut, Right and Left — pair	28/3	8/3	9/3
Jaws, Bolt Clipper, Centre Cut, Right and Left ,,	32/6	9/3	10/-
Jaws, Side Nut Splitter, Right and Left ,,	36/3	—	11/9
Jaws, Soft Chain, Right and Left ,,	35/6	10/-	10/9
Jaws, Hard Chain, Right and Left ,,	35/6	10/-	10/9
Bottom Strap — each	4/2	1/10	2/1
Top Strap ,,	4/2	1/10	2/1
Jaw Bolt (Right Side, Left Thread) ,,	1/8	8d.	10d.
Jaw Bolt (Left Side, Right Thread) ,,	1/8	8d.	10d.
Handles (pair complete with Fittings) — pair	40/6	10/6	12/6
Handle, Right, without Fittings — each	14/7	3/4	3/9
Handle, Left, without Fittings ,,	14/7	3/4	3/9
Adjusting Section (Right) and Rivet ,,	3/9	1/10	2/1
Adjusting Section (Left) and Rivet ,,	3/9	1/10	2/1
Connecting Bolt (Right Side, Left Thread) ,,	1/7	7d.	8d.
Connecting Bolt (Left Side, Right Thread) ,,	1/7	7d.	8d.
Centre Connecting Bolt (Right Thread) ,,	1/7	7d.	8d.
Section Adjusting Screw ,,	1/7	7d.	8d.
Handle Adjusting Screw ,,	1/2	7d.	8d.
Buffers, Washers and Rivets — pair	2/1	1/2	1/4
Pin between Jaws — each	8d.	—	—

All Spares are interchangeable with American make.

RECORD WORKS - - SHEFFIELD, ENGLAND

SECTION 6

CRAMPS
Pages 144-145

C. & J. HAMPTON, LTD. - - MANUFACTURERS

RECORD STEEL SASH CRAMPS

With Improved Malleable Iron Fittings.

Fig. 135.
Bar 1¼" x ¼".   Depth of Jaws 2".

Fig. 131.
Bar 1¼" x ¼".   Depth of Jaws 2⅜".

Fig. 133.
Bar 1½" x 5/16".   Depth of Jaws 2¼".

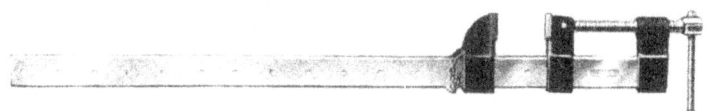

Fig. 132.
Bar 1½" x 5/16".   Depth of Jaws 2¾".

RECORD WORKS - - SHEFFIELD, ENGLAND

C. & J. HAMPTON, LTD.   -   -   MANUFACTURERS

RECORD STEEL SASH CRAMPS

With Improved Malleable Iron Fittings.

Bright Steel Bar, Square Edges.   Malleable Iron Head and Jaws, finished black.
Bright Steel Screws and Handles.
Fitted with Bar Stop to prevent Loose Shoe from being lost.
The Sliding Shoe has a Solid Steel Taper Peg.

Fig. 135.
Section of Bar $1\frac{1}{4}'' \times \frac{1}{4}''$.   Depth of Jaws $2''$.

Length of Bar	24	30	36	42	48	inches
To take in...	18	24	30	36	42	,,
LIST PRICE	11/5	11/10	12/3	12/8	13/1	each
Code Word	Ibfal	Ibfea	Ibfib	Ibfoc	Ibfud	

Fig. 131.
Section of Bar $1\frac{1}{4}'' \times \frac{1}{4}''$.   Depth of Jaws $2\frac{3}{8}''$.

Length of Bar	24	30	36	42	48	inches
To take in...	18	24	30	36	42	,,
LIST PRICE	11/7	12/-	12/5	12/10	13/3	each
Code Word	Ibiag	Ibibi	Ibick	Ibiel	Ibiga	

Fig. 133.
Section of Bar $1\frac{1}{2}'' \times \frac{5}{16}''$.   Depth of Jaws $2\frac{1}{4}''$.

Length of Bar	24	30	36	42	48	54	60	inches
To take in...	18	24	30	36	42	48	54	,,
LIST PRICE	13/10	14/5	15/-	15/7	16/2	16/9	17/4	each
Code Word	Ibdae	Ibdef	Ibdig	Ibdoi	Ibduk	Ibdyl	Ibcyd	

Fig. 132.
Section of Bar $1\frac{1}{2}'' \times \frac{5}{16}''$.   Depth of Jaws $2\frac{3}{4}''$.

Length of Bar	24	30	36	42	48	54	60	inches
To take in...	18	24	30	36	42	48	54	,,
LIST PRICE	14/10	15/5	16/-	16/7	17/2	17/9	18/4	each
Code Word	Ibeba	Ibelc	Ibend	Ibepe	Iberf	Ibesg	Ibeti	

RECORD WORKS   -   -   SHEFFIELD, ENGLAND

C. & J. HAMPTON, LTD.   -   -   MANUFACTURERS

LENGTHENING BARS for RECORD SASH CRAMPS

For **Fig. 135.**
Section of Bar 1¼" × ¼".

Length	...	...	24	30	36	42	48	inches
LIST PRICE		...	7/2	7/7	8/-	8/5	8/10	each

For **Fig. 131.**
Section of Bar 1¼" × ¼".

Length	...	...	24	30	36	42	48	inches
LIST PRICE		...	7/2	7/7	8/-	8/5	8/10	each

For **Fig. 133.**
Section of Bar, 1½" × 5/16".

Length	...	...	24	30	36	42	48	54	60	inches
LIST PRICE		...	8/10	9/5	10/-	10/7	11/2	11/9	12/4	each

For **Fig. 132.**
Section of Bar 1½" × 5/16".

Length	...	...	24	30	36	42	48	54	60	inches
LIST PRICE		...	8/10	9/5	10/-	10/7	11/2	11/9	12/4	each

RECORD WORKS   -   -   SHEFFIELD, ENGLAND

C. & J. HAMPTON, LTD. - - MANUFACTURERS

RECORD RIBBED G CRAMPS
Fig. 120

For Light Woodworking Service.

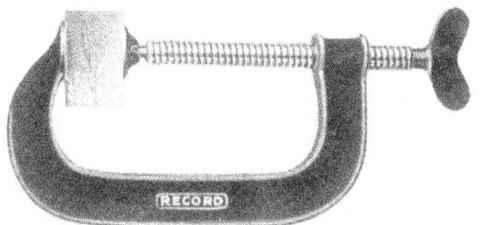

Sizes : 2, 3, 4, 5, 6, 7, 8 and 9 inches.

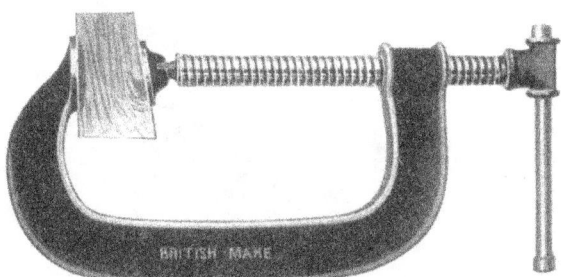

Sizes : 10 and 12 inches.

Malleable Iron Frame, Steel Screw with machine-cut square thread.

10" and 12" sizes are fitted with Vice Handles.

All sizes fitted with Swivel Shoe which adapts itself to any angle of grip.

(Code Word—Iglay).

To take in inches	2	3	4	5	6	7	8	9	10	12
LIST PRICE doz.	30/-	36/-	48/-	60/-	72/-	84/-	96/-	108/-	120/-	162/-

2" to 6" packed 3 per box.

7" & 8"   ,,   1   ,,

RECORD WORKS - - SHEFFIELD, ENGLAND

RECORD LIGHT T-BAR CRAMPS
Fig 136.

With Non-Bending Steel Bars.

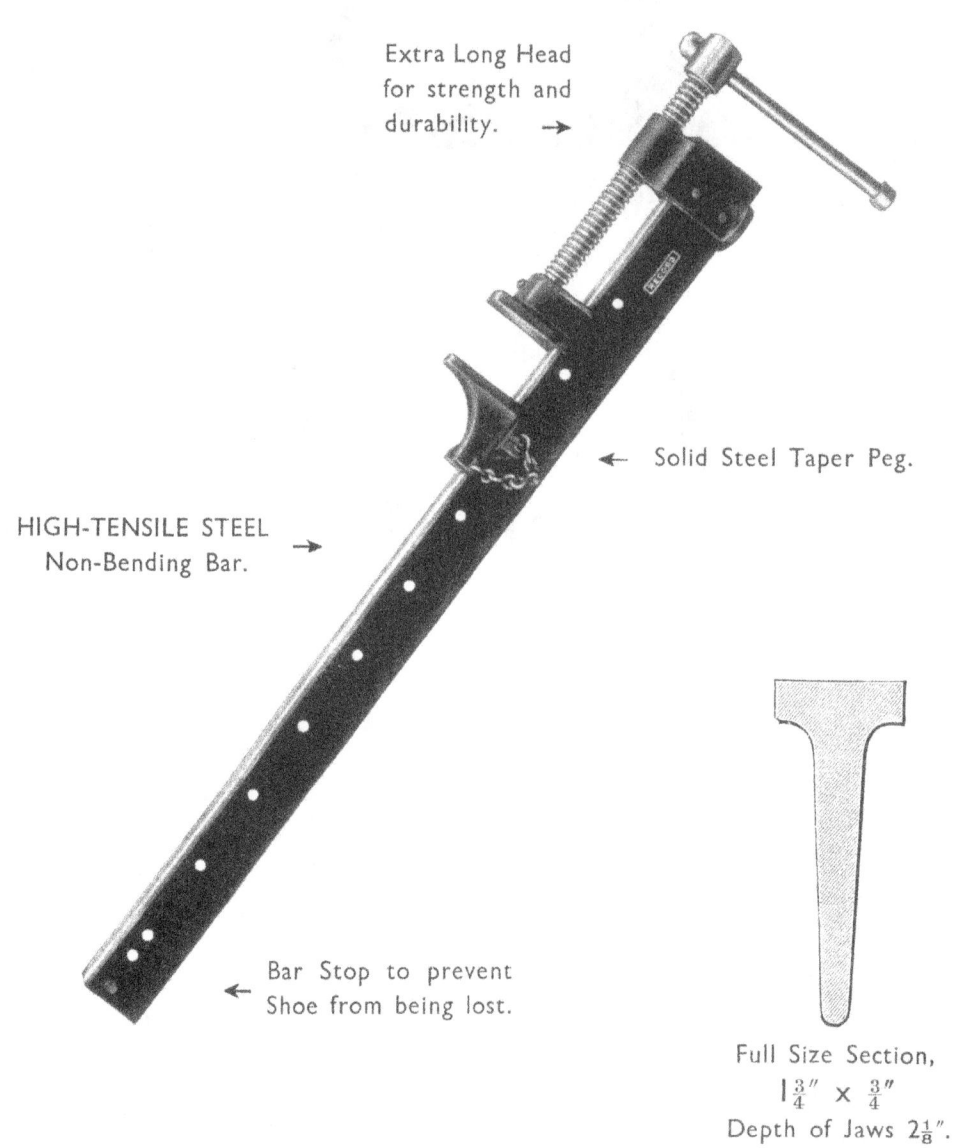

Extra Long Head for strength and durability. →

← Solid Steel Taper Peg.

HIGH-TENSILE STEEL Non-Bending Bar. →

← Bar Stop to prevent Shoe from being lost.

Full Size Section, $1\frac{3}{4}"$ × $\frac{3}{4}"$
Depth of Jaws $2\frac{1}{8}"$.

C. & J. HAMPTON, LTD. — — MANUFACTURERS

RECORD WORKS — — SHEFFIELD, ENGLAND

C. & J. HAMPTON, LTD.   -   -   MANUFACTURERS

RECORD LIGHT T-BAR CRAMPS
Fig. 136

With Non-Bending Steel Bars.

The Bars of these Cramps are made of special tough Steel of high tensile and non-bending quality, and the Bar will not bend or spring in use.

The T edges on which the Jaws slide are accurately machined and polished bright to ensure easy sliding movement.

The Head is made of best Malleable Iron, and the threaded part in which the Screw works is made extra long to give smooth working and increased durability.

Jaws are of best Malleable Iron, finished black.

Stop is fitted at end of bar to prevent Sliding Shoe from being lost.

Solid Steel Taper Peg for easy adjustment of Sliding Shoe.

CRAMPS.

Length of Bar Inches	To take in Inches	List Price Each	Code Word
24	18	14/10	Itags
30	24	15/5	Italu
36	30	16/–	Itamy
42	36	16/7	Itawo
48	42	17/2	Itbor
54	48	17/9	Itbus
60	54	18/4	Itbyt
66	60	18/11	Itges
72	66	19/6	Itgit

LENGTHENING BARS, Fig. 137, to suit above Cramps.

Length Inches	List Price Each	Code Word
24	7/8	Itcau
30	8/3	Itciz
36	8/10	Itcom
42	9/5	Itcun
48	10/–	Itdap
54	10/7	Itder
60	11/2	Itdis

RECORD WORKS   -   -   SHEFFIELD, ENGLAND

150

C. & J. HAMPTON, LTD. - - MANUFACTURERS

RECORD STRONG T-BAR CRAMPS
Fig. 138

With Non-Bending Steel Bars.

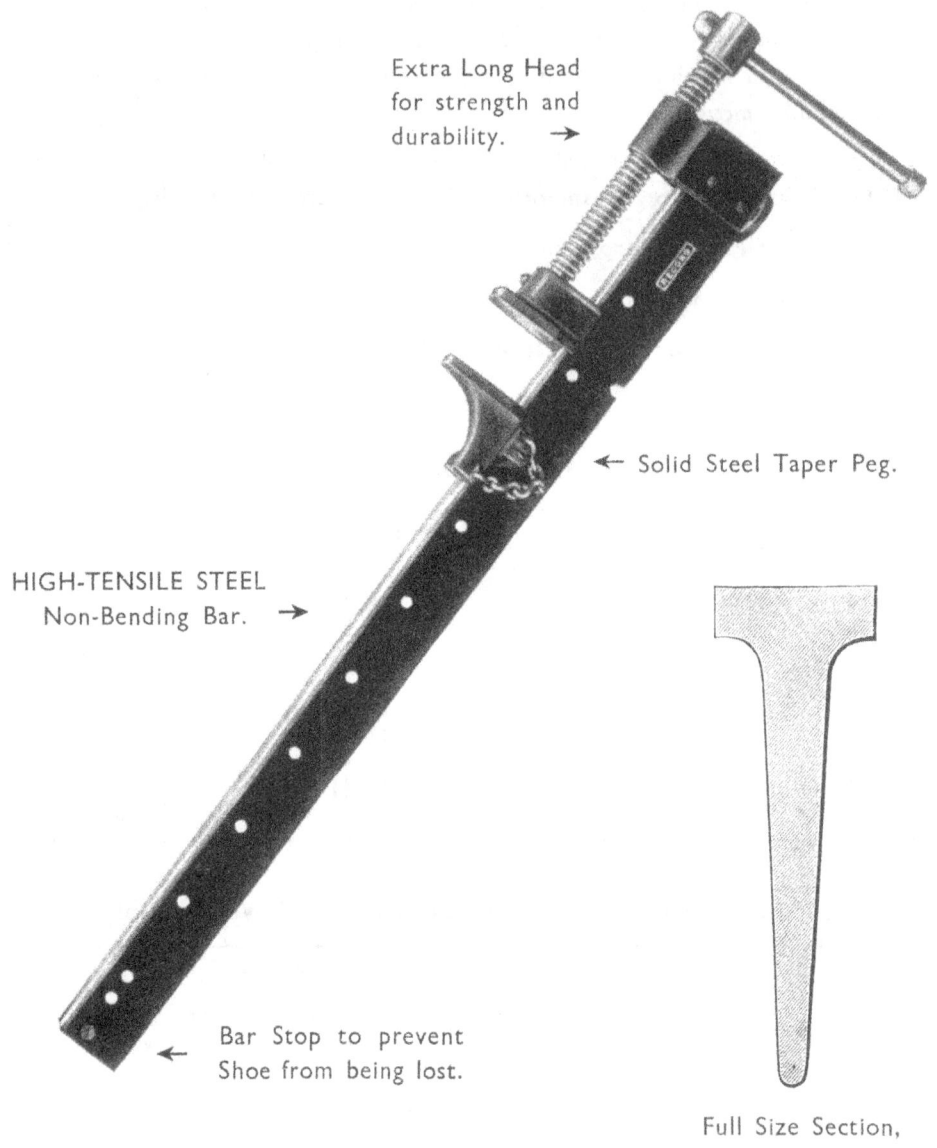

Extra Long Head for strength and durability. →

← Solid Steel Taper Peg.

HIGH-TENSILE STEEL Non-Bending Bar. →

← Bar Stop to prevent Shoe from being lost.

Full Size Section, $2\frac{5}{8}'' \times \frac{7}{8}''$
Depth of Jaws $2\frac{1}{2}''$.

RECORD WORKS - - SHEFFIELD, ENGLAND

C. & J. HAMPTON, LTD. - - MANUFACTURERS

RECORD STRONG T-BAR CRAMPS
Fig. 138

With Non-Bending Steel Bars.

The Bars of these Cramps are made of special tough Steel of high tensile and non-bending quality, and the Bar will not bend or spring in use.

The T edges on which the Jaws slide are accurately machined and polished bright to ensure easy sliding movement.

The Head is made of best Malleable Iron, and the threaded part in which the Screw works is made extra long to give smooth working and increased durability.

Jaws are of best Malleable Iron, finished black.

Stop is fitted at end of bar to prevent Sliding Shoe from being lost.

Solid Steel Taper Peg for easy adjustment of Sliding Shoe.

CRAMPS.

Length of Bar Inches	To take in Inches	List Price Each	Code Word
36	30	22/6	Itdot
42	36	23/3	Iteby
48	42	24/–	Itepo
54	48	24/9	Itext
60	54	25/6	Itezu
66	60	26/3	Itfay
72	66	27/–	Itfez
78	72	27/9	Itfim
84	78	28/6	Itfon

LENGTHENING BARS, Fig. 139, to suit above Cramps.

Length Inches	List Price Each	Code Word
30	10/9	Itnaf
36	11/6	Itneg
42	12/3	Itnoi
48	13/–	Itnuk
54	13/9	Itnyl
60	14/6	Itoba
66	15/3	Itolc
72	16/–	Itone

RECORD WORKS - - SHEFFIELD, ENGLAND

C. & J. HAMPTON, LTD. - - MANUFACTURERS

RECORD FLOORING CRAMPS

Fig. 150
Side Action.
Approx. weight 24 pounds.

Fig. 151
Top Action.
Approx. weight 28 pounds.

Cast Iron Body of guaranteed strength, Malleable Iron Fittings, Steel Screw.

Fig. 150 (Side Action).

			No.	1	2	3
To suit Joists	...	... inches		1½ to 3½	1½ to 4½	1½ to 6
Code Word ...	...	...	...	Icdib	Icdoc	Icdud
LIST PRICE ...	...	...	each	**24/3**	**25/-**	**25/9**

Fig. 151 (Top Action).

			No.	1	2	3
To suit Joists	...	... inches		1½ to 3½	1½ to 4½	1½ to 6
Code Word ...	...	...	...	Ibgaf	Ibgeg	Ibgli
LIST PRICE ...	...	...	each	**25/9**	**26/6**	**27/3**

RECORD WORKS - - SHEFFIELD, ENGLAND

C. & J. HAMPTON, LTD. - - MANUFACTURERS

RECORD "EASY" FLOORING CRAMP

Unbreakable.

No. 152.

FEATURES :

1. Unbreakable, as all parts are made of Steel or Malleable Iron.
2. Light in weight—13 pounds complete.
3. Will stand rough usage.
4. Gears are machine cut from the solid, ensuring smooth and easy running.
5. Rapid Screw Action and Positive Grip.
6. Quickly released from joist by Lever.

To suit joists $1\frac{1}{2}''$ to $4\frac{1}{2}''$. Weight 13 pounds. Code Word : lbgok.

PRICE ... **25/-** each.

RECORD WORKS - - SHEFFIELD, ENGLAND

PARTS for RECORD FLOORING CRAMPS,
Figs. 150 and 151

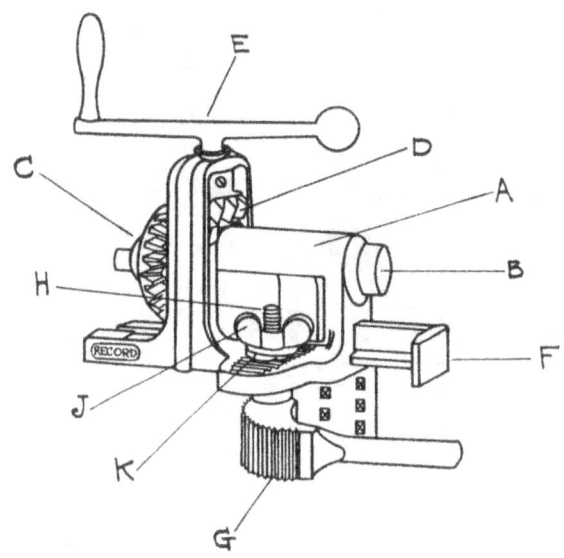

A	Body, Fig. 150, Size No. 1	12/9
	,, ,, ,, No. 2	13/6
	,, ,, ,, No. 3	14/3
A	Body, Fig. 151, Size No. 1	14/3
	,, ,, ,, No. 2	15/-
	,, ,, ,, No. 3	15/9
B	Main Screw	5/-
C	Large Gear Wheel	2/-
D	Small Gear Wheel	1/-
E	Handle	3/6
F	Sliding T-Piece	3/-
G	Lever complete with Spindle (H), Wing-Nut (J) and Washer (K)	6/6
G	Lever only	3/-
H	Spindle	2/-
J	Wing-Nut	1/-
K	Washer	6d.

C. & J. HAMPTON, LTD.   -   -   MANUFACTURERS

PARTS for RECORD CRAMPS

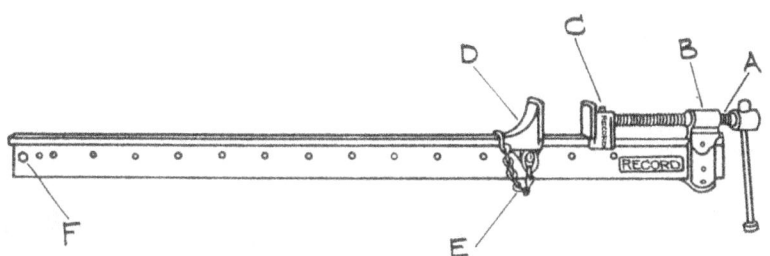

FOR RECORD SASH CRAMPS FIGS. 131 TO 135.

		For Fig.	135	131	133	132
A	Main Screw and Handle		4/-	4/-	4/9	5/-
B	Head		2/6	2/6	3/6	3/9
C	Working Shoe		2/6	2/6	3/6	3/9
D	Sliding Shoe with Peg and Chain		3/6	3/6	4/-	4/3
E	Peg and Chain		1/3	1/3	1/3	1/3
F	Bar Stop		6d.	6d.	6d.	6d.

FOR RECORD T-BAR CRAMPS FIGS. 136 AND 138.

		For Fig.	136	138
A	Main Screw and Handle		6/-	8/-
B	Head		4/9	5/3
C	Working Shoe		3/6	4/-
D	Sliding Shoe with Peg and Chain		4/-	5/3
E	Peg and Chain		1/3	1/3
F	Bar Stop		6d.	6d.

SWIVEL SHOES FOR RECORD RIBBED G CRAMPS, FIG. 120.

For	2"	3"	4"	5"	6"	7"	8"	9"	10"	12"
Per dozen	4/6	4/6	5/6	5/6	8/-	8/-	9/-	9/-	13/6	13/6

RECORD WORKS   -   -   SHEFFIELD, ENGLAND

C. & J. HAMPTON, LTD. - - MANUFACTURERS

LITERATURE

LITERATURE: Attractive lists are supplied to Stockists of Record Tools.
ELECTROTYPES for printing and advertising may also be had on request.

RECORD WORKS - - SHEFFIELD, ENGLAND

C. & J. HAMPTON, LTD. - - MANUFACTURERS

SHOWCARDS and DISPLAY BOARDS

Examples of SHOWCARDS and DISPLAY STANDS.
These are supplied with RECORD TOOLS to assist display and stimulate sales.

RECORD WORKS - - SHEFFIELD, ENGLAND

C. & J. HAMPTON, LTD. - - MANUFACTURERS

INDEX.

PLANES | Pages
Adjustable 6–14
Block 40–42
Circular 22
Combination 30–33
Corrugated Base... 9–10, 13–14
Multi-Plane 34–39
Narrow Cutter Clamping Bracket 32
Parts 54–63
Planecraft Book 47
Plough 26–29
Rabbet and Filletster 15
Rabbet—Bull-Nose ... 16–18, 21
Rabbet—Jack 15
Rabbet—Shoulder 20
Rabbet—Side 21
Rabbet—Skew 19
Rabbet—Smooth 15
Rabbet—"Three-in-One" ... 18
Router 23–25
Scrub 23
Spare Irons 48–52
STAY-SET Cap Iron ... 11–14

SPOKE SHAVES AND SCRAPERS
Scrapers 46
Spoke Shaves 43–45
Spare Irons 51

VICES | Pages
Auto 84
Auto Vice on Stand 86
Combination 94–95
Fitters 82–83
Fibre Grips for Vices 102
Garage 85
Heavy Chipping 92–93
Heavy-Duty Iron 96
Heavy-Duty Steel 91
Machine 97
Mechanics' 78–81
Parts 114–117
Pipe 120–123
Spare Jaw Plates 103
Staple 98
Steel 88–91, 93
Steel Floor 100–101
Swivel Base 80–81, 83–85, 89, 95
Table 87
Vice and Cramp Combined ... 112
Woodworkers' 105–112

DRILLS
Breast 70–72
Hand 66–69
Chucks 73
Parts 74–75

Continued

RECORD WORKS - - SHEFFIELD, ENGLAND

C. & J. HAMPTON, LTD. - - MANUFACTURERS

INDEX—*Continued.*

PIPE TOOLS   Pages
- Cutters—
    - Three-Wheel 130–131
    - Link 132–133
- Vices—
    - Chain 123
    - Hinged 120–121
    - Open-Side 122
- Stands with Pipe Vices ... 124–125
- Wrenches—
    - Chain 126–127
    - Stillson 128–129

CRAMPS
- Flooring 152–153
- G 147
- Sash 144–146
- T-Bar 148–151
- Parts 154–155

BOLT CLIPPERS   Pages
- Bolt Clippers 136–142
- Jaws and Parts 141–142

MISCELLANEOUS
- Bench Screws 104
- Bench Stop 113
- Fibre Grips for Vices 102
- Jacks—Motor Lorry 118
- Plumb Bobs 53
- Portable Vice Bench 99

ADVERTISING MATTER
- Display Stands ... 64, 76, 134, 157
- Electrotypes 156
- Literature 156
- Showcards 157

RECORD WORKS - - SHEFFIELD, ENGLAND

C. & J. HAMPTON, LTD. - - MANUFACTURERS

RECORD

TRADE MARKS REGISTERED IN ALL COUNTRIES.

RECORD WORKS - - SHEFFIELD, ENGLAND

www.ingramcontent.com/pod-product-compliance
Lightning Source LLC
Chambersburg PA
CBHW060513300426
44112CB00017B/2655